Jordan's Road

THE WAY OF THE SPIRIT IN THE HARD THINGS

LAURIE BERRY CLIFFORD

BUDDHA FROG PRESS
ASHEVILLE, NORTH CAROLINA

Printed and bound in the United States of America

Buddha Frog Press trade paperback edition:
ISBN-13 978-0-9789430-4-2

Library of Congress Cataloging-in-Publication date is available.

FOR JORDAN

TO THE ONE

When the hard things come,
they bring a fork in the road.
Then you have only two
choices: take one path or
the other. Open up or close
down. What you choose
makes all the difference.

CONTENTS

Dear Reader,

If you aren't ready to travel a hard road with me, I would encourage you to put this book down. Save it for a time when you need to know how the pain holds the grace and the grace holds the pain. I want you to know as well that because Jordan's Road is such a personal story, I have changed all first names to middle names except for my own, my husband's and Jordan's.

Love and Blessing --

Laurie

Chapter 1

❀ ❀ ❀

Our deepest fears have their genesis in the mystery and dissonance of childhood. This is true for even the most protected child of the most harmonious marriage. My deepest fear came cloaked in the baggage of our family business. Our business was thought to be "God's work," but I seemed to have been born with an allergy to it. And I observed as a young child, that when it came to the hard things of life, God didn't spare his servants. He seemed to have no scruples against chopping them up and feeding them to their enemies as tasty snacks.

I am the third of six children, three girls and three boys, born to Christian missionaries. Although missionaries populate our history books for their role in spreading Western culture, they are but a tiny segment of our society. My parents drew our family circle even smaller by choosing to become non-traditional missionaries. My father was not a preacher or a teacher or even a doctor. He was an airplane pilot.

The world of my childhood was full of sorrow and death. These were all around me in the poverty and deprivation of the people my parents had come to serve. Some Christian missionaries talked as if we were magically exempt from the ravages of evil because it was God's job to protect "his servants." I did not believe this, nor would my parents back it up. We were not poor and we were not deprived of life's essentials, but it was clear to me very young that I still had to be on guard for the hard things of life. Sooner or later, they would come my way. While I tried to prepare myself for whatever these might be, I also prayed with fervor to be spared one thing. Beyond all others, my greatest fear was that our small family circle would be fractured by the death of one member.

I have no difficulty pinpointing my happiest childhood memory. The roof of our big house in the town of Siguatepeque, Honduras, needed repairs. Yet the roofers waited to remove the tiles until late in the dry season. The rainy season arrived before the work was finished and it rained steadily for days. Everything and everyone in our house was moved to the dry addition that had replaced the small original kitchen. Now we had a big kitchen, dining room, bathroom, office and wraparound porch. For the few days we stayed in the annex, it felt to me as if we had landed in the safety of Noah's ark without all the animals. In my little-girl heart, I wanted this to last forever.

Dad couldn't fly because of the rain and Mom wasn't off saving souls. She was right there where I could see her. All the kids were home all day and, most special of all, I could hear my favorite lullaby as I went to sleep each night. Our beds were crammed together and the sweet melody I craved so much, each member of my family breathing, erupted in a symphony of sound. It was sweet music for me to sleep by, safe and secure because we all were there. None of us would die while it still rained because no one could leave the ark and fail to return.

I was spared my greatest fear until I was twenty-five, now married and the mother of two young sons. Yet when this thing I feared most came upon me, I found the One on the other side. This was not a fierce and bloody monster, ready to feed me to my enemies. Instead, this was a loving Presence that held me and cried with me and poured the balm of Spirit into my broken spaces.

In the early morning hours of July 19, 1974, my much beloved youngest brother, Larry, died in a single car crash. When my older brother, Will, arrived at my home that morning to share the sad news, he knew little beyond a few details of Larry's death and the fact that all of us would be leaving for Southern California by plane that afternoon. It seemed to me at first that Will and I were under water and he was speaking to me in speech bubbles. They burst in front of me without divulging their contents. When he left, I sat trying to understand how my baby brother, just beginning his adult life at nineteen, could be gone from sight.

Larry's teenage years were troubled. He was lost in the way so many other children of the early seventies were lost. A few weeks before his death, however, Larry made a change. He told Mom he was leaving the past behind and moving on. He made plans to attend college in the fall and seemed to be taking hold. Mom, who had spent hours on her knees by her bedside praying for Larry, felt safe enough about him to take a long trip away from home.

Tenderness for my brother overwhelmed me as I fought to absorb the new. I found childcare for my two young sons and went out to walk the summer streets outside our home in Evanston, Illinois. A small breeze wafted over me as I passed under a canopy of elms that lined our street. I thought the pain would slice my heart in two, disintegrating the pieces. I wanted to roll myself into the tiniest ball possible and store myself in a crack of bark on the nearest elm.

As I walked, not knowing where to go, torn by the pain of Larry's life and the pain of my loss, I began thinking of him as he was now. Whatever we meant when we talked about the heavenlies, he was there now. And wherever his spirit was, I suddenly knew he felt sadness for our family but absolute gladness for himself. The soft breeze caressed my face, then seemed to grow. And with it, my own spirit lifted as if carried upon the kindest of winds. I raised my hands to the sky in response and a smile of deep joy surprised my face.

Just then an acquaintance walked toward me, greeting me and asking what was going on. "My brother Larry was killed in a car crash this morning," I said smiling, much to her bewilderment. "And the thing is, I know Larry's with the One!"

I walked on, thinking I soon would focus on the pain again. Instead, the pain formed the words *thank you* inside me, contradicting my sorrow. "Thank you!" I found myself shouting aloud. "Larry knows now what he always wanted to know. Thank you! He knows!"

The pain continued this way for me throughout the next two weeks in California. I seemed to be a vessel holding deepest joy and deepest sorrow in like measure. I had thought them to be contradictory emotions. Now my heart understood the truth although my mind still couldn't comprehend it. Joy and sorrow were two sides of the same thing. Halves of the same whole. I felt it impossible now to contain the whole without experiencing both sides of it.

The details of Larry's death remained sparse as our family gathered in Orange County. Larry had stayed late into the night at a friend's house, leaving in the early morning to drive home and never arriving. His car was traveling in the fast lane when, for reasons unknown, it veered abruptly, skidding over two lanes and landing in a drainage ditch. Perhaps he fell asleep for a moment, then overcorrected. Perhaps he swerved to avoid another car or an animal in the road. Whatever the cause, no one reported seeing the accident happen and a subsequent autopsy revealed nothing amiss before the crash.

It was unusual to wear a seatbelt back then. The force of Larry's tumbling car ejected him from the driver's seat and deposited him face down in a drainage ditch beside the freeway. But not before it crushed his heart against the steering wheel. A passing driver saw the lights of the wrecked car shining from beyond the damaged hurricane fencing and alerted the authorities.

I thought, when I heard the details, that my brother's death was not a mistake. His heart had been crushed by the steering wheel, his body had been broken by the ejection from the car, and his lungs had been filled with water from the drainage ditch. Larry had been killed in three ways. Crushed, broken and drowned.

Dad was home alone when a policeman arrived to give our family the news. The pain of the officer's words rooted him to the entryway of the house. He stood there until the officer left. Then stood there still. When he finally turned, his gaze was drawn through the floor-to-ceiling windows in the living room to his rose garden beyond. There, glistening with early morning dew, was a perfect rose.

Dad had been waiting for the first perfect rose of the season and it had been delayed in its arrival. Now as he walked through the living room toward the garden, the pain of Larry's absence filled his being, settled and became part of him forever. Then he opened the patio door, stepped outside, and walked toward the rose. In those few moments, my father accepted my little brother's death and found a way to make it part of his own celebration of life. The rose was deep red, perfect indeed, and he knew that it was Larry's rose. He picked it, put it in a white vase, and set it alone on the mantle above the fireplace. There the rose remained, for weeks without withering.

Nothing about Larry's death was so straightforward for my mother. She was devastated when he was taken from her, remorseful that she had been miles away on the morning he died. "Something in me died when Larry died," she said later. "And I think nothing ever will be really hard again."

Larry died on a Friday and his body was buried the following Monday. I'd been a songwriter since my teens and often thought how rewarding it would be to write a perfect song. One in which I could find no flaw in the music, the lyrics or the way it suited the occasion. As we prepared ourselves for the celebration of Larry's life, I asked silently for a perfect song. Then I sat down with my little sister Elizabeth in her bedroom and "Kingdom Citizen" showed up.

Searching, restless searching,
Anguished for the well to fill inside.
Looking at the world and all its troubles,
Feeling your oil would never soothe the tide.
Now you're a kingdom citizen.

Chorus: Kingdom Citizen, drink from the vine,
Eat at the table spread for you.
Clap your hands, kick up your heels.
Shout! Christ is Lord at last.

How I love you, brother,
How I long to hold your hand.

Let's go walking through the meadow,
See the river flowing by.
Now you're a kingdom citizen.

Morning's come to stay now,
New day's never gonna end.
Jesus in his arms enfolds us,
Love and laughter fill the air.
'Cause you're a kingdom citizen.

The church filled on the afternoon of Larry's funeral. All seven of us Berrys sat with our spouses and children at the front of the church. Partway through the service, my two sisters and I sang "Kingdom Citizen," accompanied by Elizabeth's guitar. We sang the haunting verses through our tears and my tambourine rang out assuredly with each joyful round of the chorus. Later as the congregation sang, "Like a river glorious is God's perfect peace…," I reached for the hand of the Berry on either side of me. Then our whole family held hands and lifted them up upward together toward the heavenlies.

Our family stayed at the church as long as we needed. Then we followed the hearse to what now would become our family gravesite. Dad had purchased six plots directly under a small tree destined to grow generous with its shade. Time seemed to stop for me at the cemetery. I felt as if I could stay there forever. When our family finally left to go home, it still was to be together. Someone offered us the use of a beach house, and we left the next day for Newport.

The days we spent at the beach house reminded me of the rains in Honduras and my own personal Noah's ark. Now the pleasure of my family's company and the symphony of their sleeping did not come to me as a hedge against death, however. Death no longer was the monster that could destroy me at any moment. Instead, it was a fierce but necessary ally. It already had deposited one of us on the other side. It would come again and again, mostly without warning. Death was part of my life now and reason for me to celebrate life through my tears.

My brother Larry stepped into the next room twenty-six years ago. My father followed him twenty years later. Although I still am alive on this earth, my loved ones arrived in heaven only a split second before me. The truth is that in heavenly time, in no time, nothing separates me from them. Their spirits live outside of time now and because they live where there is no time, my spirit is with them already. The deaths of my beloveds have widened my perspective and deepened my understanding of life. I no longer fear time because I understand that I, too, am already living in eternity.

For two years, I grieved Larry's absence on this earth in the way that the memory of his earthly life was ever present with me and the death of his body never far from my mind. Some months after his death, I came down with an illness that turned out to be parainfluenza. I was so sick I thought that I, too, would leave my body. I was face up on my bed one morning, listening as a friend escorted my children away to care for them, when I understood for the first time in my life that I am not the One.

This understanding was completely new to me, even though I had been raised from infancy in the Christian faith. Although I had separated early from my earthly mother, understanding she was a wholly different person from me, somehow I had never separated from my heavenly mother. And I did not understand that the One has an existence wholly apart from my own.

At the moment I understood this bedrock principle, I felt my own life to be useless as I was too sick to live it. *But the One isn't sick,* I thought, and then continued this line of reasoning to see where it would lead me. *And when you are tired, the One isn't tired. And when you miss the mark, the One doesn't miss the mark. And when you are weak, the One isn't weak. And when you are angry, the One isn't angry. And when you despair, the One doesn't despair.*

My heart understood then that I am a created being and that the Divine is so much greater than the human as to be almost unfathomable. I had known myself as part of the One, but now I understood that the Divine is not tied to my human state. This knowledge of the One as apart from me settled deep within my being. In that brief moment, I was given an unending inner awareness of the One that is worthy of all praise, simply by virtue of Being.

I reminded myself that lovers of great art live their whole lives simply for times when they can sit before their favorite works and gaze upon that which fills their souls with delight. I told myself I would be this way with the One. I would live for the times when the earthly veil parted and I was allowed to gaze upon the Divine. Allowed to fill myself with inexplicable beauty. A joy came into my heart then that remains to this day. It was a wellspring of gladness that has stayed with me for forty-two years now.

I know I glimpsed the sovereignty of the One that long-ago morning. Since then, my heart has understood that I, too, am part of that Mystery. I have entrance to the Wonder any time I present, without expectations, the will to see it. I am heartened by the knowledge that the dance of Life is not primarily about me. My own human life is but a small part of Life itself and because of this, I am allowed to stand back whenever I have need and appreciate the Greater.

Something beyond price was birthed within me that day. I know that in my human self I am not the One, and yet the One is closer to me than my breathing. More often than any lover of art gazes upon a treasured work, I can behold the treasure of my heart. The One requires only the surrender of my human will to disperse the fog between us, and it is in this exchange that I find my purpose. The old creed is right. I was created to behold my Creator and to enjoy this Communion forever.

Chapter 2

❀ ❀ ❀

The One never fails to use the hard things of my life to deepen me and create spaces within me for Spirit. The only thing needed from me is to say yes, moment by moment, choice by choice. Whether the hard things come to me through my own choices or seemingly by random fate, the One always is about transforming the fallout and turning it into Grace.

I want always to be aware that I have a choice. I can trust and cooperate or I can turn my back and refuse. I can say yes at an elemental level to what life brings, no matter how difficult this seems, or I can hide my head and play the child. There were times when I was younger, however, that I could only scream and ask for my terror to be interpreted as a cry for help. Some of the hardest things in my life have come as the result of my own choosing. These are choices I survived only by holding on to the One as fiercely as possible. These were choices that took a long time to redeem.

My marriage was difficult for me even before the beginning of it. On the day of our wedding, March 28, 1970, I wanted nothing so much as to hop on the first bus heading east out of town. I wanted to escape and let my parents clean up the aftermath. Dad always told me, however, that the problem with running away is you have to come back sometime. I knew this to be true and I knew Wayne, my husband-to-be, always would tug on my heart. Instead of running, I went to the church.

As I waited alone in a small dressing room to the right of the sanctuary, my bones felt like water to me. Every fiber of my being screamed the word, *Run!* Then when I thought I could stand it no longer, Spirit descended on me and I heard ten words clearly in my mind. "It won't be easy, but it will be all right." With this faint promise, I walked out of the dressing room, into the sanctuary, and married Wayne.

Years later, people still remember our wedding and tell me how full of grace it was. Our early years of marriage were anything but graceful, though, and nowhere near "all right." Wayne and I fought so often that my little sister refused to ride in the car with us. Once when she had no other alternative, Elizabeth offered us a quarter, big money for small chores in those days, if we wouldn't fight.

Into this scene of domestic un-bliss, a strange prophecy found its way. One day, a friend came to us with a story. Becky told us she had received a vision. At first, she described an active volcano. This was a metaphor I knew well in our marriage. Then she talked about the volcano becoming dormant, settling down and providing rich soil for a garden to grow. Finally, she painted a lush picture alive with loving words. It spoke of a verdant place where birds sang and all nature lived together in harmony.

When she finished, Becky moved on to the interpretation. "I believe my vision was for you," she said. "I think the volcano is your marriage. One day it will calm down and when it does, a beautiful garden will grow. On that day, your marriage not only will bless the two of you and your children, but it will bless others as well." Becky's prophecy seemed unlikely to me, but I tucked it away next to the words Spirit had spoken to me on our wedding day. I pondered these two prophecies for years.

Like mine, Wayne's greatest fear began with the letter D. It wasn't death, however. It was divorce. I had mentioned divorce often over the years, but the closest we'd come to it was one day when a physical feeling came over me of no longer being able to breathe. Despite years of marriage counseling, Wayne still wanted too much of me. Late one Saturday afternoon, thirteen years into our marriage, I asked him for a trial separation.

The next morning I didn't go to church with Wayne and the boys. Wayne told me later that he tried to stay in the Sunday service. But finding himself too emotional to participate, he went outside to sit on a low wall and weep. As he wept, Wayne heard these words, spoken clearly within. "Do you love Laurie?" the voice asked.

"Of course, you know that I do," Wayne responded.

"If you really love her, you'll give her what she needs," the voice said. "Even if what she needs is to not be with you."

By some miracle of Grace, Wayne not only heard but accepted this. On the way home that Sunday morning, he told our three children that Mommy and Daddy were going to live apart for a while. When they got home, the boys burst through the front door and threw themselves into my arms. "It's not true what Daddy said," they pleaded with me. "Tell us, Mommy, it's not true!"

I was stunned that Wayne, who didn't have much of a relationship with his sons at the time, would take it upon himself to inform them of my request. This was not the man I thought I knew so well. I didn't understand his motivation until later when we were alone and he explained what he had heard.

I calmed the boys down by telling them I would talk with each individually, starting with the youngest. When it was George's turn, our middle son walked into the room, closed the door and faced me. "It's okay, Mommy," he said, his face so sweet and his voice so innocent. "I just talked to God and he told me not to worry because it isn't going to happen."

Although I didn't yet know what Wayne had heard, I knew better than to step on my child's faith. While still certain the separation was necessary, I didn't press my opinion on our nine-year-old. Instead, I told him I would be glad if he was right. George walked out of the room a happy boy.

Wayne and I did not separate then. Those few whispered words from Spirit to Wayne gave us breathing room for another four years. Then I admitted I was helpless to change our marriage and left it. All my trying hadn't made the prophecies come true. Wayne was forced to face his own greatest fear. And like me, he found the One steady and strong on the other side of his fear.

When I finally left, it was in June of 1987. By this time, the kids were in therapy and something the child psychiatrist said jolted me into action. He said, "You know that you don't have a husband, don't you? You have four boys. And your sons are here because of their father. I firmly believe children are better off in a single-parent home where adults are adults, the rules are clear and the home is in peace, than in a two-parent home where chaos reigns."

The two younger boys and I went to stay with my parents for a few days while I figured out what to do. Tom, the oldest, was in high school. He stayed with Wayne to finish the school year. When I awoke my first morning at the Berry Patch, I felt like Pilgrim in *Pilgrim's Progress.* It was the scene where Pilgrim reaches the cross and the burden on his back, one he's carried all his life, breaks free and rolls off at the foot of the cross. The first thing I thought as I walked out to Dad's rose garden was, *I won't disappoint anybody today.* The long years of feeling that I wasn't enough for my husband finally were over.

I remember feeling desolate later as I pondered my choices, however. All three of the cottages at the Berry Patch were full at the moment, which meant we had only floor space for sleeping. I soon found myself living with the two boys in a small, hot, borrowed, concrete block track house, miles away from the spacious country home Wayne and I had built near San Diego. To give myself time in a more conducive environment, I took George and Kenny on a long visit back to Illinois.

While we were in Illinois with my best friend Beth, I pondered my marriage well. Several months later, I flew home, leaving the boys with Beth, to ask Wayne for a divorce. The first time I walked back into our house, I was astonished. The place I had loved so much barely resembled the home I had known. Formerly bright with its high ceilings and natural lighting, the house now felt dark and dingy. The imagery that came to me was one of cobwebs sprouting in every corner. Tom complained immediately that all his dad bought for them to eat was milk and bread. Both had lost weight and looked like street people to me. I decided to remain where I could feed Tom at least, rented a small apartment in town, and sent for my other two children.

When I told Wayne I wanted a divorce, he responded, "If that's what you need. But I want you to know it won't be because of me that our family isn't together." He proceeded to become Jesus to us then for the months we lived in the apartment. He made sure all our needs and wants were provided. He befriended the boys. He became gentle with me, undemanding and most respectful of my personal space. I learned he had started counseling while I was away, both with a professional therapist and with his priest. In time, I found I liked the way he was with me now although I still loved being single. And I still wanted not to be married to him.

I made plans for the three boys and me to leave San Diego County and move to San Luis Obispo. I loved the central coast of California and I thought it a good place to start over. Plus I had editorial work at the time and could take the job with me wherever I wanted. After so many years of continual stress, everything seemed perfect in my life. I felt truly happy and although I cared for Wayne, I did not think I loved him. My plans were in progress when a most unexpected thing happened. A great fear came upon me. For three days, it was as if my bones were made of water. I didn't know what could be causing my distress. The fear wouldn't go away, though, and I finally decided that as with prophets of old, it had been sent to instruct me.

I called Wayne on the phone and asked him to come over. When he arrived, I inquired if his offer to be the one to vacate the house was still good. He said that it was. I told him about the bones-turning-to-water thing and said, "I'm willing to trade living spaces and give our relationship another try. But if you accept and it doesn't work, you lose everything. I'm taking the house, the kids, your money; and you won't have anything left."

I wanted my words to sound as stark as possible, in case he needed to think twice. But all he said was, "Okay." We made the switch, dated for several months, and I began to see in Wayne a gentle man with wonderful qualities. We soon renewed our marriage, coming together as two free and separate people who truly wanted the best for one another.

Our marriage has not been the same since. We are still the same flawed people we always were, but the ground rules have changed. Each of us is responsible for resolving his or her own issues and for finding his or her own happiness. Some of my closest friends also have had difficult marriages. All of them have been divorced for years because their husbands did not know how to be Jesus to their families when their wives finally insisted things had to change. Out of all these couples, only Wayne took the servant role. Only my husband incarnated Jesus for his family. Wayne is the one who saved us and now has an unbroken family to bless.

Chapter 3

❋ ❋ ❋

I think I've lacked a certain commonsense wisdom in my life. No sooner was our marriage and family on safe footing than I decided it was time for us to give back. This took the form of hard-to-place foster children. Among them was a small, blonde-headed, blue-eyed pixie named Donna and she undid me completely. But not in a good way. Nobody could keep her. She had been in seven placements in three years. I didn't think I would survive my first year as her mother.

Donna was only five when we got her and unless you've been there, it's hard to understand how someone so little could create so much havoc. This in the life of a grown woman who regularly handled teenage delinquents with grace. The year that followed purged me of any do-gooder notions about foster parenting. I was exhausted, beat down, and wanted nothing so much as to get this child out of my life. The only thing that stopped me was a deep-seated conviction that if I didn't make a stand for her, no one would. Finally, after debating it with myself again one long evening, I decided to send her back to the foster agency. I awoke Wayne at midnight to tell him my decision. He turned over, thought about it, and said, "It's up to you, of course. If you can't do it, you can't do it." But he added, "I'll never believe it was right, though, if you send her back."

I went upstairs after that to sit beside Donna's sleeping form and wait. *How can you send her back,* I asked myself, *if Wayne never will believe it was right?* Easier for him to say this, of course, as he left the chaos every weekday and went off to work. But was there something more for me in his words?

Until then, I had felt a confused sympathy for Donna mixed with a healthy dose of amusement and irritation over her outrageous behavior. Layered between these two emotions, however, there was an aching resentment over the way my life had changed. I had been young and lively before Donna's arrival, or so I told myself. Now I just felt old and tired, both inside and out.

I sat beside Donna for an hour that night. As I watched her breathing in and out, Spirit gave birth to her in my heart. It wasn't much, only a tiny embryo. But I clutched it and sat with it and clung to it. Then I heard familiar words. They were the same ten words Spirit had spoken to me twenty years earlier on my wedding day. "It won't be easy, but it will be all right."

I got up after that, went back downstairs, slid into our bed and whispered the Spirit words to Wayne. "It won't be easy, but it will be all right."

Life with Donna continued apace after that. Not much changed. I had a dream about her that proved to be prophetic, though. In the dream, we were on vacation and staying in a hotel that somehow also was a hospital. Wayne and I were sleeping upstairs. Kenny and Donna were sleeping in downstairs bedrooms off a large foyer. In the middle of the night, I heard Donna screaming and rushed down to see what was wrong. Two men in white coats had her between them, and they were struggling to make off with her.

Donna was fighting as usual, and carrying on as only she could. That two grown men were not enough to handle her didn't surprise me. I rushed to her and reached her at the same time as Wayne and Kenny did. Then all four of us fought off Donna's abductors together. When that ordeal was over, I said, looking at Donna in my dream, "Well, I bet you never thought your obnoxious behavior would get you anything good. But tonight it kept you safe and with your family."

The next morning after I entertained Donna with my dream, she said, "Oh, Mommy, I wish it would really happen!" And I knew what she meant. She wanted all of us to rescue her and finally bring her home. And, in time, we did.

A few years later, Donna was taken away from us through a misunderstanding with a young social worker who knew little of our situation. The new worker showed up at Donna's school without warning and brought her home only to get some of her things. Both Donna and I started crying, at times wailing hysterically, as the social worker instructed Donna to pack. Donna went up to her room, refusing to put anything in her suitcase except for one change of clothing and one hair bow. It was her way of telling me that she would be gone for only one day.

I had instructed her to "be good" so she waited patiently at her new foster home for one day. Then when she wasn't returned to us on the second day, she began to act up. On the third day, she took matters into her own hands. She found a metal pole and tried to crack a birth child's head open. It's easy math when you're a foster child. Split a birth child's scalp? Bye-bye, foster home! After this, the do-gooder social worker called Donna's therapist and asked for advice.

"You have three choices," the therapist said. "You can put her in a home with no other children and an adult who can watch her twenty-four hours a day. Homes like that are hard to find. You can put her in a hospital. But she already has proven she deteriorates in institutional settings. Or you can send her home to the Cliffords where she belongs." Donna was back home on the fourth day. Her obnoxious behavior finally had gotten her something good.

San Diego County no longer seemed like a safe place for our family to me, however. Within months, Wayne and I sold our home and moved to live for a while at the Berry Patch with my parents. A half-acre property at the base of the San Bernardino Mountains, the Berry Patch had a stream running through it, a covered bridge, and three small cottages built in the 1920s. We stuffed ourselves into the front and the back cottages while my parents continued living in the middle cottage next to the stream.

What followed, in short order, were calamities of biblical proportion. First, there was an earthquake. Next, there was a fire. It came within inches of the property and spewed ash to every corner. Driving rains followed, pounding ash on the surrounding hillsides into mudslides that covered the property. I went from wondering, *When will this end?* to simply asking, *What's next?* All four of our children found themselves at change points. Personal difficulties overwhelmed Wayne and me as well. I worked long hours as editor for a business that was faltering. Wayne suffered from exhaustion, driving two hours to his old job every day and two hours back. It felt to me that, slowly and deliberately, everything was being taken away. I remember walking around in a nice comfy sweatshirt one morning, my hands clasped together in the pocket, and thinking, *Well, I still have my jacket!* Then I started to laugh. Human beings cling to security, wherever they can find it.

On July 24, 1994, Dad gave us a gift of words on the occasion of a family wedding reception. He looked tired and drawn as he took time before prayer to say:

There is a concept that is fundamental to the Christian life. That is the idea that Jesus Christ came to this earth to die and thereby model for us the way we should live. You might think that dying is not a great

way to live. We all know something about living, yet some of us in this lifetime would prefer not to think about death. But the concept of dying daily is a good perspective for what real living is all about.

The way of Christ is a call to daily dying, but with each dying comes a resurrection. It is a daily breaking of our hearts with a soon mending of them so that this living for Christ may go on and on. Know this: there is no danger in having our hearts broken as long as we soon turn to Christ and accept the sweet balm of God's mercy and grace.

That summer of 1994 was one of the hottest on record in California. My teeth began to ache and I soon learned that I needed several root canals. I was so miserable in the heat that I sought solace in Tom's apartment with central air. I was down the road from the Berry Patch and I didn't see Dad after that as often as I had when I was living on his property. I do remember one particular occasion clearly, though, a precious moment with Dad.

The two of us went out to lunch away from the heat, and when he brought me back to Tom's apartment, Dad asked if we could sit in the truck for a few minutes. Then with the motor running and the air blasting, my father gave me a blessing.

The times Dad decided to give one of us a "blessing" were blessings themselves. Sometimes the blessing was a twenty-dollar bill. Other times it was a prayer. Sometimes, it was simply words from his heart. My father's blessing that day seemed to be none of these to me. More than anything, it felt like a good-bye.

He told me first how proud he was of me and how close he had felt to me all my life. Then he thanked me for coming to stay with him and Mom at the Berry Patch. "No matter how many things have gone wrong with your stay here," he said, "I always will be grateful you came. It means more to me than you can know."

When it was my turn to speak, I thanked him and apologized for the chaos our arrival seemed to have generated. "I am sorry for all the stress," I said, acutely aware of his history of heart attacks.

Dad looked over at me and grinned. "Well, you know," he said, "if it isn't one thing, it's another." I knew what he meant by that. I knew he was telling me that life is life and, no matter what, "I choose you."

I saw Dad again after that, but I don't remember where or when. Someone who knew the walking disaster our life had become asked me how I was coping. "At least, nobody's dead," I said, laughing.

Two weeks later, I walked into my parents' cottage and found my father's body.

Chapter 4

❀ ❀ ❀

Mom left the Berry Patch on a Monday for a short stay in Pasadena. Wayne ate dinner with Dad on Tuesday evening. Kenny gave his grandpa a hug before bedtime that night, inquiring if he wanted to keep our Rottweiler with him for the night. Dad said he'd better not. Although his doctor had just given him "a clean bill of health," he was unusually tired. He thought he would sleep better with only Junkyard, his little asphalt-colored poodle, by his side.

Junkyard and my dad were inseparable. Dad had named her *Sombra*, Spanish for *Shadow,* but he kept forgetting what he'd called her. He teased her about being an "old junkyard dog" and the name stuck. Dad went to sleep with Junkyard that night. His pattern was to sleep with the radio on, wake early to read the morning paper over breakfast, then set out to supervise his small gardening business. His clients were mostly widows, many of them lonely for company. While his helpers did the heavy work, Dad and Junkyard both visited with the widows and both politely accepted treats.

Tom spent Tuesday night at the Berry Patch and was supposed to meet me at the apartment the next morning. When he didn't arrive by ten, I decided to look for him. No one answered the phone at the Berry Patch so I drove the mile to the property, parked my car outside the gate, and looked through it for Tom's car. When I didn't see it, I got back in my car and drove away. As I was leaving, however, the picture I had just seen focused in my mind. Dad's truck was still in the driveway, next to his cottage, and the morning newspaper was still just inside the gate where it had been tossed. This picture was wrong. Not the way it was supposed to be at 10:00 on a Wednesday morning.

I gave myself a short lecture on not breathing for the people I love and reminded myself of the day before. I had followed an ambulance from the apartment all the way past the Berry Patch just to make sure it didn't turn into my parents' property. *This is just the same thing,* I scolded myself. *You'll turn around and go back and everything will be fine and it will be just like it always is. You're always checking up on the people you love.* But then I couldn't remember the last time I'd seen my dad and I told myself I didn't care if I was being silly. I turned the car around and went back to check on him.

The first thing I heard after I rounded the corner leading to the back door of the middle cottage was the sound of Dad's radio blasting. It should have been off by now. Another sign things weren't right. Two thoughts played against one another for space in my brain. *Daddy can change his routine without asking you!* That competed with, *Is this really it? Is this the scenario you've envisioned for so long?*

I had known for some time that I would be the one to find my father's body after he left it. I didn't know how I knew, but I knew. I had practiced in my mind's eye what would happen and how I would respond. I would find him in one of two positions. He would be sitting up in his chair or lying down in his bed. Either way, I would sit beside him quietly, praying for strength, telling him how much I loved him, saying my good-byes, and thanking God for his life. Once again, real life didn't meet my expectations.

I called for Dad as I entered the back door. "Daddy!" No answer. "Daddy!" I walked into the tiny kitchen. It was empty. No sign of breakfast on the table or in the sink. "Daddy!" The radio came from his bedroom. "Daddy!" My heart turned to lead. But for the radio, the cottage was filled with an eerie silence. I had never felt so alone.

I walked to the open bedroom door and peered cautiously around it. Junkyard was running around in circles on my parents' bed. I called to her, but she refused to come. She just kept running around in circles. I poked my head further into the doorway. Then I saw Dad's body. It was slumped on the floor against the side of the bed. His right hand was on the hose of a portable vacuum and his left hand was propped against his left cheek.

He looked so defenseless with his body gleaming in the sunlight that poured through the bedroom windows. All I could think was that I wanted to help him. My whole life he had helped me. He had been the emergency person, the one I went to when anything needed fixing. Now he was broken and I wanted desperately to fix him. I stepped over to put my hand on his back. "Daddy?" I asked. "Daddy?" His body was warm, but his voice was silent. I felt no breath in him and I stepped back, aware that I wanted to cry.

Then I thought, *What if he's not dead? What if someone can help him?* I remembered a newscast where the announcer said the worst thing people do is not to call 911 immediately. I went to the phone then, but I had trouble punching out the three numbers. Something was wrong with my fingers. They didn't work right. And my hands looked like somebody else's hands. After several tries, I managed the emergency code and an operator came on the line. "I think my father's had a heart attack," I said. "I think maybe he's dead."

When I knew that paramedics were on the way, I made my own emotional 911 calls. Whatever the outcome of this day, I did not want to go through it alone. I called Wayne's pager with our emergency code and then dialed my older sister, Helen, in Pennsylvania. She answered the phone immediately. When I heard her voice, I began sobbing. "I think Daddy's dead," I said. "Pray for me because I'm here all alone and I don't know what to do. And please call everybody else." Next I called my mother at the mission office, a two-hour drive away. I told her only that paramedics were on their way because "Daddy is on the floor and I can't get him up."

When I hung up, I went back to the bedroom and peered through the door. Junkyard was curled up next to Dad now, licking his face. "Daddy?" I called. "Daddy?" He had fallen in such an unusual position, wedged between the heater and the bed. I had learned CPR as a foster parent, but I did not think myself strong enough to get him up on the bed without help. There was no room to unwedge him and stretch him out on the floor.

I didn't know where I should be. Should I be out on the road hailing the ambulance as it approached and making sure it didn't miss the property? Should I be staying near the phone in case they couldn't find us and called for directions? Should I be with Dad in case he needed me? Since I couldn't decide which to choose, I tried to do all three. I ran from the house to the road and back again, crying and flapping my arms. In between my crying and flapping, I made the sign of the cross and said my siblings' names. Over and over I repeated this ritual. *Sob...flap...sign of the cross...Helen, Will, Eddy, Larry, Elizabeth.*

The Berry Patch, usually so full of life both human and animal, was completely silent until the ambulance arrived and the paramedics took over. By some mercy, Dad's priest was on call that day and received a page from the police department. He arrived at the Berry Patch not knowing the emergency was his beloved friend and former senior warden. Wayne and Tom arrived separately soon after. They were followed by Mom, Elizabeth and her husband,

and Kenny, in that order.

For his children, their father's body was the most familiar thing. He was an emancipated male long before it was fashionable. He did most everything, including flying an airplane, with a baby hanging off one arm. He liked to tell the story of flying with me when I was a toddler. He took me above the cloud cover where everything looks pretty much the same. As we cruised along, I stood beside him, my left arm draped around his neck. Finally noticing the scenery wasn't changing, I asked, "What are we hanging around here for?" This story always made Dad laugh, but the truth is that just hanging around with my dad was what I liked best. I wanted nothing more than to be wherever he was. I still can close my eyes and trace the landscape of his brown, freckled body and it still is the most comforting image I can summon.

Dad's Episcopal church was overflowing for his service, filled with people and love. We sang our best songs and told our best stories. When it was my turn to speak, I said, "A few weeks ago, I found my dad at the back of the Berry Patch. He was standing by the woodpile, holding a cup of coffee and smiling out on the mountains behind the property. When he realized I was there, he said, 'I don't know what it is about this time in my life. But sometimes, I get so tickled over being alive that I have to buy a donut and a cup of coffee. Just to celebrate!' And with that, he danced a little jig around the yard."

I stopped to let his friends laugh and then I added, "This is my wish for each one of you today. I want you to feel glad just to be alive. I want you to dance a jig for life in general and for nothing in particular. In everything you do, please find occasions to dance!"

After that, people who loved my father, some of whom I did not know, stood throughout the church and told stories about him. Mostly they told how he had loved them and treated them with such kindness. Then finally the church was quiet as my nephew Martin played his guitar and sang words and music he'd written.

For I've cried and you've answered me,
I've asked and you've given me everything I need.
Let my love increase,
Make me one with your Word,
Make me one with your peace.

After we celebrated Dad's life in the sanctuary of the church, we held a reception in the fellowship hall. Then we took his casket to the hearse and followed it to our family gravesite in Orange County. Under the green canopy that workers had set up, our family celebrated Dad's life once again. Time seemed to stop. Before we said our last good-byes, my sisters and I sang "Kingdom Citizen," changing the word "brother" in the last verse to "father." Then I watched as the body of the person I trusted most in this world was lowered into the ground.

Chapter 5

❀ ❀ ❀

My father died on a Wednesday. I stayed strong until Monday. Then our family had a picnic at the Berry Patch that afternoon and I told my mother I felt as if I were drowning in a swimming pool. I had a physical feeling of my lungs filling up with chlorine water. That night I became desperately ill with a strange pneumonia, although it didn't show up as anything on the x-rays. My father was dead and my human lifeline to everything good no longer existed on this earth. My inner self was drowning and my body was only cooperating.

I was so low in the first months after his death that I could barely care for myself. During this time, the only reason I found to be alive besides my children was that somehow my presence made Wayne happy. I felt as if my entire life had been wasted, as if I had squandered everything I had been given, and nothing was left to justify my space on this earth.

Wayne was as perfect a comfort as a human being could be in the days after Dad's death. It's a tricky thing to give solace to a person in deep grief. The slightest misstep can be monumental. But Wayne navigated those waters with me as if he had been born to them. I think it helped that he loved my father deeply and had considered him to be his best friend.

My father died on August 10, 1994, and by the end of November things were so bad for me I thought they couldn't get worse. One morning, I could stand the grim, tight world inside myself no longer. Yet, shell of a human being or not, Wayne still wanted me alive. After all he'd done for me, I didn't want to question his choices. Instead of a hundred other scenarios that played out in my imagination, I spoke aloud to the One. "This emptiness inside me is so awful," I said, "that I can think of only one thing to do. It's so horrible that all I can do is to thank you for it. Whatever it means and whatever it's good for, thank you for giving me this rotten life."

Two weeks later, Spirit began healing me. I came upon a passage in the Old Testament that gave me hope. As can happen, the words came alive and attached themselves to me with great promise. In Deuteronomy 8, Yahweh talks to the Israelites about their forty-year trek through the desert. It was a relatively short distance they had to travel from Egypt and yet it took them forty years because they were led around in circles. Yahweh could not let them enter the promised land until they were ready to inhabit it. This wasn't a punitive fact. It was a matter of fact. And it is the same for all of us. None of us can enter our own promised land until we are ready to be in it. And getting ready usually takes lots of desert experience.

Deuteronomy 8 reviews the benefits of the desert years. Then it goes on to describe the wonders of the promised land, all pure gifts of Grace. Finally, the passage closes with a warning: *Beware of saying in your heart, my own strength and the might of my own hand won this power for me,* Yahweh says, *because if you do you most certainly will perish.* On the day you reject what you have learned in your desert years, saying it no longer is necessary, on the day you believe you have found a better sustenance than the daily bread provided for you, on that day, by definition, your stay in the promised land is over and you are back in the desert.

I was forty-six when I found Deuteronomy 8 and I told myself that I, too, had wandered in the desert for forty years. I had taken on the persona of a mother with my younger siblings when I was six and I had been mired in my own story ever since. *But now,* I thought, *I am standing on the brink of the promised land.* Spirit poured through me like a holy river for three days then. At one point, I was given a glimpse into my future. I received six specific things. The words came to me unexpectedly and I rushed to write them down on pink sticky notes. I pondered these words for a while and then read them to Wayne.

All the personal prophecies given to me that day have proven true. The most instructive thing about them, however, is that none of them turned out like the projections I had made in my head. Everything looked far different from the way I had imagined it. Not long ago, I found listed elsewhere what I had written on the sticky notes and was amused to see that I had begun the process of editorializing immediately. I had recorded specific words from Spirit and then rolled directly into my own stuff. Almost no time had passed before I began forming my own opinion of what essentially was none of my business.

One of the prophecies was that our family was coming into a "time of plenty." I followed this quote with instant elaboration. I imagined healthy chunks of money coming in. Instead, I was taught how to wait for my daily bread and to discern the difference between my wants and my needs. Another of the prophecies had to do, in part, with my writing. I imagined, of course, an instant bestseller. Instead, I learned to work on my stories. They always had come easy for me, but I learned to polish them until they shone. One of the prophecies was prosaic, however. It said that we wouldn't "have to fight cars that break forever." This made me laugh.

One night three years later, I heard Spirit tell me something about my writing. This time it was about an autobiographical work. It was specific and hammered itself into me all night long. I wrestled with it, tossing this way and that in our bed trying to get away from it. There were few things I wanted less than to write a book-length work of nonfiction. And as with all the prophecies given to me before, this one could not be pinned down.

Later, after I unburdened myself with Wayne and with my sister Helen, I decided to leave it alone. It was clear to me now that if I tried to do anything about it myself, I would fail miserably and waste a lot time being unhappy. Instead I gave my permission for the book to come into being, if it was in fact to be, and then as much as possible, I forgot about it. I knew that if I ever did write an autobiographical book, I would need to experience the most incredible joy in the writing. The chances of this seemed on par with winning a lottery I hadn't even entered.

No matter what your temperament, there is a great gift in surrender to the One. If you are someone who kicks and screams all the time, it can make you feel wonderfully serene. If you are a person who lumbers through life under a cloud of depression, it can make you climb high to walk above the clouds. No matter who you are, it can give you cause for rejoicing. This all has to do with purpose. You were born for a reason. You were embodied to begin on this earth a heavenly dance that has no end. When you make the connection your heart desires, when your human spirit comes alive with divine Spirit, you can say and truly believe that nothing else matters.

In the summer of 1999, I began to feel pregnant with a book different from any I had ever written. The genesis came from my grandson Justice. He made a startling observation about me. In working this up into a short essay, I found myself welcoming a longer work based on my life and not clothed in the guise of fiction.

Funny Elbows

Justice was a tough and tender boy who melted me and took me back to my own little boys, now grown men but still tough and tender. When he was two, my grandson realized there was something different about my elbows. I had enormous arms and when I straightened them, each had not one but two large dimples set like twins on either side of the elbow.

Justice was fascinated with muscles. He worked out often with his daddy whom he adored and he proudly demonstrated his "muscle" to anyone who might admire it. Since Justice's elbow was his muscle, he decided that my strange elbows must be unusual muscles. When we visited one another, he would tug at my shirtsleeves and ask me to hike them up so that he could get a good look at my "muscles."

By the time he came to visit his Nana and his Poppa shortly after his fourth birthday, however, Justice knew the truth. Nana was fat, and people didn't think fat was a good thing. During the first couple of days, I could tell he was studying me from a new perspective and from time to time, he would pat my fat, my chins or my tummy or my arms, and ask little questions about my appearance.

"Nana, why is your tummy so big?" he asked. I gave him the standard answer passed down from my father. "Honey," I said, "I'm the smartest person I know and I just don't have room in my head for all my brains.

That's why my tummy is so big. It's where I keep my extra brains."

Little did I realize that my light-hearted answers only deepened my grandson's dilemma. He knew his grandmother was fat, but all his inquiries led him to the belief that she was unaware of her predicament. No one had given her the bad news. As much as it pained him to do so, he finally decided it was up to him to give me the sad facts of life in our culture.

One day we were driving by ourselves in my car. I was in the driver's seat, of course, and he was buckled up in back behind the front passenger's seat. From his vantage point, he had a box seat view of my right elbow. We drove quietly for a while. Then with a deep sigh, he broke it to me.

"Nana, you have funny elbows," he said firmly. "And people will laugh at you." He stopped to let the bad news sink in, then sweetened it with a grace note. "But I won't laugh at you," he said, "and Jayne and Jaylene and Aunt Sarah won't laugh at you," naming the relatives we were on our way to visit.

I watched his sweet little face in the rear view mirror and wondered how to alleviate his distress. "You won't laugh at me because you love me, Justice, and that's what really matters," I said, hoping he wouldn't spend the rest of his childhood grieving my funny elbows. "The people who do laugh at me don't love me. That's why I don't care if they laugh."

He thought about this for a moment and a look of compassion came over his face for this clueless old woman. "Oh, but Nana," he said, "when people that don't know me laugh at me, it makes me really sad."

We were quiet again in the car, the air filled with empathy. I was unable to counter his wisdom. I had funny elbows and all my grandson's love could not stop people from laughing at me. And it mattered.

Yes, it did.

I was fifty when Justice shared his wisdom with me. I loved being fifty and decided to celebrate my exalted state by writing my "fat, fifty and fabulous" story. My reaction to the first draft of any new book is similar to my response to each of my newborn babies. Ecstatic! It must be a hormonal thing. If I could bottle my book-and-baby chemical for selling, I'd be a wealthy woman. This lack of perspective allows me no initial measure for the true ultimate value of any of my books.

I was in this kind of love with *Funny Elbows: Fat, Fifty and Fabulous* when I remembered my propensity for messing things up. As a defense against it, I formulated a daily ritual. On my morning walks, I would stop at a certain spot and hold my hands open, lifting them upward to the One. Then I'd say, "My hands are open and I will for them to remain this way." In doing this, I gave conscious permission for my plans to fail if necessary so that higher plans could succeed.

This was a radical act for me. My mom brought me up on a story about a woman who prayed an unwise prayer. She prayed for God to try her by fire, figuratively speaking, of course, and God supposedly allowed her to be burned to a crisp, literally speaking, and yet survive. I certainly knew enough not to pray for trial by fire or any such gruesome thing. I was an MK, a missionary kid, and MKs knew, almost by instinct, that you don't give God a blank check. If you do, you won't get married or have kids and you will be shipped off to Siberia with no warm clothing and with only a coffin in which your body can be returned home. I did not want this to happen to me, so until I was fifty, I never trusted enough to offer any blank checks.

Chapter 6

❀ ❀ ❀

I never knew exactly why my mother-in-law scheduled routine, non-invasive surgery in mid-December 1999 instead of waiting until after Christmas. I imagine she wanted to feel better for the holidays and thought the surgery would help. No one expected complications. Wayne talked with his father after the operation and everything had gone fine. The next day when he called his mom in her hospital room, however, something had changed overnight. Vera was in such pain she could talk only a few minutes. By the following day, her lungs were filled with fluid and she was in ICU on a respirator.

As his mother's condition deteriorated, Wayne flew up to Northern California to be with her. When he called home saying Vera's doctor wanted permission to perform a tracheotomy and insert a feeding tube, I kept my counsel. "What does your father want?" I asked him, aware that his mother, now in her eighties, would veto this decision if she could. Vera's way with me was sticking to small talk, but she had deviated from this choice more than once by sharing her end-of-life wishes with me.

"Dad seems to think there's still hope for her to come out of it," Wayne said. "I guess what he says most clearly is that he isn't ready to lose her. I feel for him. He's so lonely and he doesn't know how to do anything around the house."

"Then your dad already has made the decision," I told him. "He knows he isn't ready to lose her."

Vera's condition weighed heavily on me as the new year began. She was an elegant lady who, for most of the time I'd known her, seemed physically preserved in her fifties. She didn't appear to change much until she turned eighty. In the last two years of her life, she had aged noticeably and didn't welcome it. "Eighty is enough," she told me. "I don't see much point in living beyond this. Except for..." And we both knew the "except for." She didn't want to leave my father-in-law alone to make his way through his last years without her.

Wayne came home, days went by, and I began pondering what I owed Vera. Not as a mother-in-law but as one woman to another. Although I didn't want to be the one asking the hard questions, I finally decided that I needed to advocate for her.

"There are questions to be asked before your mom stabilizes enough to be kept in this half-life indefinitely," I told Wayne. "If that happens, I don't know how we'll forgive ourselves. I feel like I'm just standing here, knowing a train wreck is about to happen and not even trying to stop it."

Wayne agreed with me and we left almost immediately for Paradise. Ironically, this was the name of the Northern California town where Vera was being kept alive/not-alive in the hospital. As we drove, we talked about the impossibility of what we needed to accomplish. Our only solution was to ask for gifts of grace and direct intervention.

Throughout the years, the men in Wayne's family had difficulty maintaining peace with one another. Now they would need to make the most important decision of their family's life and make it together. If any of them resisted, Vera would continue in a vegetative state. I thought it would take a miracle for them to come to unity. And although I had faith for many types of miracles, I didn't have faith for this one.

Wayne and I arrived in Paradise late on Saturday night. He attended church with his family the following morning. I stayed back, grateful for a time of quiet to gather myself and prepare for the trip to the hospital. I felt more inadequate for this task than I ever had felt before. As I sat alone in the guest room, I understood clearly that I had no resources within myself. Guiding this family toward the termination of Vera's life was not something I could do on my own.

Finally, I found peace in one plan of action. *There is only one thing you know how to do that might help,* I told myself. *Go to her room and pray in Spirit for as long the hospital staff allows you to stay. After that, leave and come back. Pray in Spirit for as long as you are there and for as long as they let you be near her.* I left for the hospital after this, aware mostly of all I didn't know.

It's at moments like these, although I've never had another moment quite like this one, that I find myself wanting a mother around to do the grown-up things for me. Then I remember that I am a mother and a grown-up and now's the time for me to do the mother/grown-up things for others. I knew from family legends that Vera had made the hard decisions when it was time for her own mother to die. Now it was my turn to do the same for her.

The sequencing of events leading up to Vera's release from her body was my clearest experience yet of understanding a crucial principle. It is not the quality of the One speaking that prevents me from hearing, but the quality of my own listening. As I walked into the Paradise hospital, I wanted nothing so much as to listen more deeply than I ever had before. I wanted to be for my mother-in-law everything she could no longer be for herself. And perhaps because she hadn't granted me many ways of reaching her in the past, everything within me wanted to find a path of service for her now.

Grateful for my simple plan of action, I followed a hospital volunteer down the labyrinth of hospital corridors to a small waiting room next to Intensive Care. All I needed now was a way to sit beside Vera and begin praying silently in Spirit. "Press this red button," the volunteer said. "When a nurse answers, tell her who you are and why you are here."

I did as advised and was surprised to find myself admitted promptly into the ICU. As I looked for Vera's room number, I asked silently again for help. The help first came in the form of Vera's nurse and after that, help never stopped coming as soon as I needed it. Vera's nurse ushered me into a room where a very old woman was perched in a high bed. I didn't recognize the woman.

"Are you Vera's daughter?" the nurse asked.

"I'm her daughter-in-law," I said.

The nurse nodded. "I'm concerned about your mother-in-law," she said. "I got to know her before she had to be sedated like this. I've been taking care of Vera for a while now and I've grown fond of her. She's a feisty old gal."

I smiled. "I know she is." It was nice to refer to Vera this way.

"Are you close to her?" the nurse asked.

"I guess that's a yes-and-no kind of answer," I said. "But I do know what she would want right now. My husband and I drove up from San Diego to ask the hard questions that the rest of the family seems unable to ask." I decided to go for broke. "You say you've grown fond of Vera. Do you think the right thing is being done by her?"

I thought I saw Vera's nurse back away from the silent figure in the high bed then, but perhaps I only imagined it. And when she finally spoke, I thought her voice was lowered. "Have you spoken to her doctor?" she asked.

"I just got here," I said. "I haven't spoken to anyone."

"I really can't tell you anything until after you've spoken to her doctor," the nurse said with her mouth. But her eyes told me something different.

"How about if I talk and you let me read your body language?" I asked.

She nodded.

"I guess I'll tell you how Vera felt about being hooked up to machines like these and kept alive," I said, going on share what I knew of my mother-in-law's wishes. "Maybe it would be okay if there was reasonable hope she could go home eventually and be herself again. But I need to hear from someone who knows that there is."

I watched the nurse's face as I spoke, especially her eyes, and the way she held her arms positioned as I spoke, the tension in her body. "I need to know if it's at all reasonable to expect Vera to get off the respirator and go home. Without a feeding tube or any other type of life-support."

The nurse's voice was silent yet the rest of her body spoke volumes. Finally she said, "I'm sorry that I can't help you right now."

"I understand," I said, wanting to thank her for advocating so eloquently on Vera's behalf. "I know now what I needed to know."

"You must talk to one of her doctors then," the nurse said. "I'll bring one to you as soon as possible." After that, she motioned me over to Vera, introducing me to the machines and to the figure in the high bed that I still couldn't recognize.

"Be with her. Talk to her," the nurse said. "Perhaps she can hear you. The hearing is the last thing to go." She demonstrated what to do by talking to Vera, touching her hands and her face, showing me it was all right for me to become acquainted with my mother-in-law's altered body.

I believe Vera's fate changed in the few minutes I spent with a nurse who had come to love her. I simply focused on praying silently in Spirit, listening deeply for what was next, and then doing the next thing. The next thing always was something gentle. I never had to push myself on anyone or force anything to come into line. I listened harder than I had ever listened before in my life and as I did so, the details of Vera's release from her dying body unfolded. It was as if I were turning the pages of a novel and learning the plot paragraph by paragraph.

I soon came to understand that my mother-in-law had become enmeshed in hospital politics, caught up in hierarchies of power. I can't describe the details of how everyone, hospital staff and family, came to unity on disconnecting Vera from her life-support systems because, largely, it's not my story to tell. I can say it was like being part of a medical thriller, however, with plots and subplots revealed at just the right time for me to advocate on Vera's behalf. By the time I left Paradise on the third day, I knew that I had been part of an extraordinary jigsaw of events, all cooperating to bring Vera the peace she needed. And in all of it, the greatest miracle of all to me was that the four men in Vera's life turned toward their common center and worked together for her good.

I left for home on Tuesday knowing that I would be back soon with our children for a celebration of Vera's life.

Wayne told me later that the four men gathered around Vera on Thursday, held hands and prayed for her, then watched as she was disconnected from all life-support systems. When I heard this, I knew that wrong had been put right and the gentle yet persistent urgency I'd felt about the details had been validated.

Chapter 7

❀ ❀ ❀

The year 2000 ticked off one family tragedy after another. Vera died in January. Soon after, my brother Eddy arrived at our house in crisis. Eddy was different from the rest of us. Our parents believed his brain was damaged at birth or by a high fever at the age of two. He was physically beautiful and active, but his cognitive abilities developed at their own pace. The best way to describe Eddy to someone who didn't know him was to say the words "Rain Man." His most defining characteristic, however, was a determinedly happy personality. While more "able" people complained about this and that, Eddy had a lock on the contentedness thing.

At one point, Eddy had lived with us for seven years. During that time, I wrote a short essay about him.

My Brother Eddy

My brother Eddy doesn't know to come in out of the rain. He is task-oriented. He leaves the house promptly at eight in the morning to stand at the bottom of our long driveway and wait for the bus that takes him to his sheltered workshop. If it starts to rain, he doesn't consider his options. He just stands there, resolved like the postal service to complete his task regardless of the weather.

Our family has puzzled over the mystery of Eddy's life in bits and pieces since my parents first realized their fourth child with the shiny brown eyes was "different." Now society calls him "special." Nobody else I know makes a ritual of folding dirty laundry just so and then carrying it to the hamper, piece by piece. This, and a hundred other things, makes him different. Nobody else I know is so determined to enjoy the small things of each day either. This, and a smile that warms you in places you didn't know existed, makes him truly special.

Before Eddy came to live with us, he was on a ranch in Arizona. He lived there with other "handicapped" people. I understood the need for him to leave his parental home. I had teenagers who were trying to make it on their own, and I prayed nightly that they would. After you make the break from your parents, it's important to find a home of your own. The Arizona ranch, however, was never "home" to my brother.

When we invited Eddy to come live with us, we

brought him "home." Later, I asked Eddy the difference between Michael's House, a board-and-care home where some of his friends lived, and home. We were driving into town and he took only a moment to think about it. Then he looked over at me and said, "Home is better."

I smiled. "Yes, I know we all like home the best," I replied, "but what do you think the differences are?"

Wanting to please me as always, Eddy took a long time before answering again. Then he cleared his throat, frowned with concentration, and said, "The difference between Michael's House and home is...that home is better!"

We both smiled. It was true. Home is better. And that's the only important difference. End of story.

When Eddy lived in Arizona, I thought about him at the appropriate times. I sent cards and letters, made phone calls, and had him as a guest in our home once or twice a year. But he wasn't my "problem." He wasn't my privilege either. Now that he was living with us, the privilege of my brother's company far outweighed the problems it presented. I functioned as the brains for both of us. It was up to me to be smart enough to scout the territory ahead, to keep us both one step in front of his meandering biochemistry if I could. But Eddy controlled the happiness thing. The only time it threatened to leave his grasp was when his own mortality made itself known. A stomachache or an earthquake could panic him. Then we would sit together and remind ourselves that death was only a doorway to the next thing.

I wanted to be Eddy's caregiver for as long as I could. In my mind, this included helping him facing his only true fear, the deaths of family members and finally his own. Eddy grew up with Larry, two years younger than himself. Eddy wished they both had made it to adulthood. So did I. But I wouldn't have traded one brother for the other. Not even if I could have.

Once when Eddy was in a downturn, strutting about his bedroom like a mechanical soldier and saluting all four walls, my mother told me a good friend had said it would be a "mercy if God took Eddy to his final home." My mother wondered if her friend might be right, if it might be a relief to give up our journey through the complicated maze of brain damage, manic depression and obsessive-compulsive behavior that troubled Eddy's life.

I knew she had shared this with me out of concern for my own sanity. I was the one who took Eddy's hand now when he walked down these dark corridors. But I felt her words smothering me and I wanted to run for the nearest window to gulp in fresh air. My mother's friend did not understand that although I was my brother's "care-provider," he provided care for me as well. I found that my brother made me happy for no particular reason. Eddy was childlike, but he was not a child. We both valued his independence. I didn't want to be his mother. I just wanted to bask in his joy. He didn't want to be my son. He just wanted me to tell him when to take an umbrella to work and under what conditions he should put it up.

Some traditional societies gave people like Eddy elevated status. It was believed their mysterious rituals were communications with the gods. Of course, we now know better. But I liked to think it was true. I liked to think there was a special purpose to my brother's wacky chemistry. That somehow, in the cosmic scheme of things, the "counters" and "checkers" had purpose to their work. When Eddy was busy with trivial statistics, like naming the price and history of every item in his room, I liked to imagine this was just as important as the words I put down on paper or the machines my husband repaired for high-tech companies.

The only thing I really learned as I grew older was that I didn't know much and never would. Maybe the world would fall off its axis if it weren't for the people who busied themselves with "useless" rituals. Maybe they were the ones who made the world go 'round. How could I know? How could anybody really know? Maybe if God in an act of "mercy" took them all away, we would have nothing left. I knew I would feel empty if God took my brother Eddy away.

After our father's death in 1994, I couldn't hang on to Eddy because I was barely hanging on to myself. He lived with our mother then for several years until her aging body and his own wandering chemistry made it too hard for them to stay together. Then Eddy went to live in a Christian board-and-care home.

Following my mother-in-law's death in 2000, a random thought began popping up in my mind. *They say things come in threes.* I told myself this was an odd thing to be thinking and didn't take the phrase to heart. Still, I found the thought coming to me as an unbidden stranger, yet carrying no dread.

I went back to my writing after Vera's death in January, hoping to concentrate on another draft of "Funny Elbows." Then I met with the agent I had picked to represent the book. She liked my writing, but our understandings of life's deeper purposes didn't mesh. I left confused as to why I had pursued this particular person. The thought came to me again that *things come in threes* and I told myself, detached from the idea but playing with it, *Okay, that's two. This is a death of sorts.* The following week brought news that Eddy had suffered a complete nervous and physical breakdown. With this, I told myself the abstract notion of threes had been satisfied. Vera, the agent, and now Eddy.

It was February 4, 2000, when I received a frantic call from my mother. "Something's terribly wrong with Eddy," she said. "They can't get him to eat or drink anything. If it keeps going this way, he will die. I don't know what we'll do, but I want you to know I'm not asking you to take him." I finished talking with Mom, hung up the remote phone, and continued sitting on the couch in our living room. The past six months had been particularly difficult ones for Eddy. He was more erratic in his behavior than usual and had lost weight. Still, I had been to his yearly review the week before and things seemed back on course. But now this.

Several phone calls later, the news still was grim. Eddy appeared to be having a complete physical, mental and emotional breakdown and nobody knew why. Finally, the staff at the care home called paramedics and Eddy was taken to the emergency room. I pictured Eddy taken away in an ambulance without family to comfort him and I could feel his terror. *It's as if he's falling over a precipice,* I told myself, *and there isn't anybody to stop his fall.* I imagined him going over a cliff, hanging on to scrub brush on a mountainside with only one hand. I knew I was the only one in the world who might pull him back to safety. My siblings didn't know Eddy in the way that I did and none of them had my long history with his care. My mother could help, but she wasn't young or strong enough to rescue him by herself. Knowing I couldn't let Eddy fall without trying to help him, I paged Wayne with our emergency code and waited for his call.

Eddy was released to us from the ER later that day. His difficulties were determined to be mental and not physical, as if the two can be separated, and so he wasn't admitted. When Wayne and I arrived, Eddy was standing beside his bed, a vacant look in his troubled brown eyes. Wayne drove on the way home and I sat in the back with Eddy, praying and trusting I would know what to do if he became violent. He trembled a lot, but seemed to accept that he was coming to stay with us. On the way, he sang a song our mother sang to him with the words, "Jesus loves you and me." Eddy changed the words to "Jesus loves Vanna White," a game show personality on whom he had a crush. It encouraged me that he still could make me laugh, even though he wasn't trying to be funny.

When I got Eddy home, I discovered he had lost most of his bodily functions. He could walk a few steps with help, but he couldn't use his hands for anything. He could talk if pushed to do so, but mostly he was silent. While his problem-solving skills never were great, he always was able to take care of his physical needs. Now he had no control of his bowel or bladder.

I couldn't get him to eat that first night, but I coaxed him into drinking by making him a "suicide squeeze" and giving it to him through a straw. One of Eddy's rituals was to go to a mini-mart and mix as many flavors from the soda machine as possible into one glass. We called it a suicide squeeze. It comforted me now that he still responded to this concoction.

It always has been clear that nursing is not my calling. Yet I spent the next several days figuring out how to manage my brother's care. I needed to do everything for Eddy, to anticipate his needs hour by hour, because he couldn't tell me anything. His communication skills were below that of a newborn baby's as he couldn't even cry to get my attention. Eddy was just about as helpless as a human being can get.

Something wonderful and mysterious happened to me as I cared for Eddy, however. A quality of love I hadn't experienced before flowed through me. All my life I had been good at giving because I tended to be clear about what I was getting in return, most often the satisfaction of my strong sense of justice. Now there seemed to be nothing for me to gain from my brother's care, however. Eddy was so far gone that I couldn't imagine him getting "better" in any reasonable sense of the word. The giving I experienced now was something completely new to me. It was the most tender, the most loving, the most broken I ever had felt in my life. Wayne remarked on the way I was with Eddy and how blessed he felt by it. "I know," I said, "and it blesses me too."

I found myself hoping for small things. That Eddy would respond to me by eating one more bite. That I would see his shiny eyes for just a moment in place of that haunted, vacant look. That for a split second, he would do what he'd always done against so many odds, that he would be happy. I watched myself during those days and wondered who I was. Who was this person that spent her time feeding this man, and bathing him, and changing him? I wondered at how this kind of love could flow through me as I watched myself walk Eddy around and talk to him and think of little things for us to do together. I knew for a fact that this was not Laurie's human love. And I had to conclude this kind of love came to me as a gift, unfiltered, from the One.

My own love was a fixing love, sometimes bulldozing those closest to me in my intense desire to fix things for them. The contrast between my love and the One's love was stunning to me. I learned the One's love is an abiding love, not a fixing love. I found it's much more important for the One to abide with me than to fix me. And I understood the fixing, when needed, comes of its own accord as I live in the abiding.

I felt closest to the One when I prayed with Eddy at night, tucked him into bed, and reminded him that he could call for me if he needed something during the night. It was as if the space between our two human selves was erased then. I knew Eddy wouldn't be able to call for me, but I believed I would know, even before he tried, if he needed my help.

Before Eddy crashed, I had made plans for myself. I would see *Funny Elbows: Fat, Fifty and Fabulous* through to publication. Then I would go about the country letting people know how wonder-filled it was to be fat, fifty and fabulous. To me, *fat* was a metaphor in our society for *imperfect*, so I thought almost everyone could identity with what I had to say. *Fifty* scared some people as well. I thought it would be fun to explain how both "fat" and "fifty" could be "fabulous." Now that my path had changed, however, I would stay home and care for my brother. No matter how empty it might seem for me personally at times, the One would supply all the love I needed. I'd find meaning in something I never had imagined and when it was over, years from now, I would be different, changed in some essential way for the better.

I spent three weeks taking care of Eddy. Then he put his hands around my neck and tried to choke me. We were alone in the house when it happened. I'd just given him a bath and was drying him off. He lunged at me and pinned me against the bathroom door. When it was over, he seemed as surprised by it as I was. At first this was good news to me. When I called Wayne, however, he explained it was terrible news. "If Eddy doesn't even know that he's hurting you, he could kill you without any awareness of it," my husband said. Then he made me promise to put Eddy in bed with the rails up and leave him there until he could get home.

That evening Wayne and I got Eddy ready for sleep together. As we were putting him back in bed, Eddy came after me again, his hands going toward my throat. Wayne pinned him back on the bed and explained the facts of the situation to him. Eddy again was surprised by what had happened and roused himself enough after Wayne's lecture to apologize.

"I'm sorry, Wayne," he said.

"I forgive you, Eddy," Wayne told him, "and don't worry. It won't happen again. I'm not going to let it happen again." Then Wayne ushered me from the room and told me I no longer could care for Eddy by myself.

"I think what he really wants to do is just lie there and die, honey," Wayne said. "You keep coming in and disturbing his plan. You make him eat and drink and get up and take walks. As much as he loves you, you are the one who keeps him from tuning out the world. And right now all he wants to do is to tune everything out. He'll keep coming after you until you leave him alone."

Eddy went from our home back to the same ER. From there, he was sent to a psychiatric hospital, then back to a regular hospital, then to a nursing home, then on to a long-term hospital. Finally, he came to rest in a nursing home near our mother's apartment. It didn't seem to matter to Eddy where he stayed. He was shut down, lights out, closed for business. Nobody knew exactly why, although everybody had a guess, but Eddy had decided it was time to die. And he was busy trying to accomplish it.

So this is the third "death," I told myself, believing erroneously that I was witnessing Eddy's slow death. First Vera, then the agent, and now Eddy. *So it won't be my greatest fear,* I told myself. *It won't be the baby.* And I forgot all about *threes*.

Chapter 8

✾ ✾ ✾

Jordan began his life in his mother's womb unexpectedly. Much to our surprise, Lynn, who wasn't planning another pregnancy just yet, found out she was pregnant with her third child. When our middle son, George, and his family visited us over the Christmas holidays, Lynn seemed buoyant both physically and emotionally. They had agreed to call their new baby boy *Jordan,* although his middle name was the source of controversy. George wanted to name him *Peace.* Everyone else thought it odd to saddle a boy child with a girl-sounding name.

Lynn experienced signs of premature labor in mid-March and our family began preparing for Jordan's arrival before his official due date of May 7, 2000. Sonograms confirmed that he was healthy and already three and a half pounds. The goal was to keep him in the womb, through medication and prudent behavior, until at least thirty-six weeks when he could be allowed into this world. He would be small, at five or six pounds then, but red-faced and vibrant.

The last week in March was earmarked for Wayne and me with a trip away from home to celebrate our 30th anniversary. We planned to visit Cambria, one of our favorite spots along the Central California coast. Almost at the last moment, though, I asked Wayne if we could drive up to George and Lynn's home in Northern California instead and stop in Cambria for only two nights on the way back.

Lynn and I had shopped happily together for baby things in December and I was scheduled to be with her again after Jordan's birth. Still, I had never felt my grandson kick and I felt the loss of time with Lynn in the days before her baby was to be born. I thought of my own babies just before they were born and how I almost always could locate a foot or a hand for someone to poke and play with. I thought if I were with Lynn for a couple of days, she might do me the same favor.

When Wayne and I arrived at her home, Lynn was standing at the kitchen sink looking tired and dazed. We soon learned she'd spent the day in the birthing center of the hospital where she worked as a labor and delivery nurse. Her doctors were trying to prevent premature labor again. This wasn't as worrisome to her as it might have seemed though. She had been in and out of labor for five weeks with her son Justice. He was born at almost thirty-seven weeks, happy, healthy and weighing seven pounds, eight ounces.

Lynn wanted to distract herself from thinking too much about how long this might go on and when the baby would come, of course. We spent time together over the weekend doing other things and not talking much about Jordan's soon arrival. To my disappointment, I didn't get to feel my grandson move before Wayne and I left for our Cambria stopover on the way home. I wasn't concerned about Jordan, though, certain his birth would be like his brother's. When the greatly anticipated and now impossible-to-predict day arrived, Jordan's birth would be normal and uneventful.

Nothing could have been further from the truth. Lynn did not threaten to go into labor again. But on Thursday, April 6, she noticed that she was going to the bathroom a lot. She seemed to be losing fluid even though her water hadn't broken yet. This gave her a disquieting feeling although she had just been to the doctor and everything seemed fine. No obvious cause for concern. Jordan's heartbeat was strong and he was big enough to be born now without complications.

Lynn called the doctor's office anyway and spoke to one of them. He reassured her Jordan was all right. After that, she tried to keep busy, wanting not to think so much about her impending delivery. Jordan moved mostly at night, so it didn't surprise her entirely when he was quiet during the day. Not wanting to worry anyone else, Lynn kept her growing apprehension to herself.

Lynn worried in her bed on Saturday night, uneasy because she no longer felt the baby move. She had phoned her doctor again, but again she was told things were fine.

The baby was settling, getting ready to be born. Lynn whispered as she dozed throughout the night, "Move, little darling, move," but her belly was still.

My first warning that something was wrong came in the form of two dreams, although I didn't connect either one of them with Jordan at the time. It was only later I realized what I had known. My father came to me on Saturday night in the first dream. It was a traveling dream where I went from place to place, but my dad always was in the background. And for the first time in almost six years since his death, he was not okay in a dream. Instead, he was sad and silent and swollen.

I finally slept again early Sunday morning, only to have a most disturbing dream. I was bottle-feeding a live baby, holding him in my arms and delighting in his sweet presence, when I realized he had two faces. His second face was that of a dead baby. I arose from my bed deeply troubled. As I readied for church, I pondered the meaning of both my dreams. I had no sense of mortal danger, though. For me, dreams about babies always had to do with my inner life and it made sense my dad would show up to confirm this.

Miles away, Lynn kissed George on Sunday morning and headed for the hospital, promising to be home soon. George stayed with their two children, allowing the kids a normal morning routine. *After all,* Lynn reasoned as she drove, *I'm just going to listen to Jordan's heartbeat. To reassure myself everything is fine.* Then she thought she felt the baby move and almost turned back.

Wayne and I took our time getting home after Sunday

morning service. We stopped for fruits and vegetables with no sense of urgency that we might be needed at home. When we pulled up to the house, our daughter, Donna, was standing on the front lawn with the remote phone in her hand. "Mom, it's George," she called. "He says it's an emergency!"

I bolted from the car, but didn't connect the emergency with Jordan. He was all right. He would be in our arms any day now. As I took the phone from Donna, I heard George sobbing out words I couldn't comprehend. "We need you to come now, Mom," he said. "The baby is dead."

Something was wrong with the receiver. I knew it. I never could hear right on the remote phone. Especially out on the front lawn. Too much static. I had to get closer to the base station. Better yet, I needed to find a real phone. One that connected to its base with a curly cord.

"I can't hear you," I said. "Hold on a minute. I have to get to a better phone." Rushing to my study, I discarded the hated remote and reached for the real phone. This one would tell me something better. Anything. Just not that incomprehensible thing. "Okay, I'm on a better phone," I said. "I think I can hear you now. What's wrong?"

"The baby is dead, Mom." My son's voice came to me from 740 miles away. "There's no heartbeat. They've done two sonograms. We need you to come, Mom. They say the baby is dead."

"Oh, George!" I still seemed to be having trouble hearing. "Where are you?"

"We're home. I kept trying to call you, but you weren't

there." His voice sounded so weary. I wanted to reach over the miles and hold him tight. "They sent us home. Lynn has an appointment to induce labor in the morning."

"Oh, honey!" I couldn't feel my body. "We'll leave right away."

"Dad, too?"

I glanced back at my husband who was standing behind me, hearing only my side of the conversation. "Dad, too," I said, knowing nothing could keep him away. "We'll both be there just as soon as we can."

"I need to ask you for two things, Mom."

"Anything."

"Call people before you do anything else and ask them to pray."

"I will!"

"And the other thing, we've talked about it, Lynn and I. I'll just tell you and leave it up to you. We don't want the baby to be buried here."

"Okay," I said, knowing what they wanted. George was stationed in Northern California with the Coast Guard and it was a temporary home. They wanted the baby to be buried in our family gravesite, next to my brother and my father.

"I'll just leave it up to you," he said again. "I have to get back to Lynn now, Mom. I love you. Tell Dad I love him. Tell Tom, Kenny and Donna, too."

I began my telephone marathon after that, comforted by the fact that Kenny was at college up in Northern California already. He could get to George and Lynn in only four hours and they would have family with them before either set of parents could arrive. When I reached Kenny, he said, "I'll be in the car in five minutes."

I kept my phone list on my desk. As I began going through the names, they fell in one of two distinct categories for me. When I came to the name of a person who wasn't known as someone who prayed, I skipped the name temporarily. People known to pray are attached to other people known to pray. I wanted the prayers of family and friends to multiply in the shortest time possible. I wanted them to call their families and friends for prayer. I wanted prayer to bless George and Lynn from the north, south, east and west, from upside, downside and all-around-side.

"Pray for a miracle," I sobbed as I hurried through the list. "Pray the doctors are wrong, that the baby is born alive. And pray for grace. Call your prayer people and ask them to pray."

When I got hold of my mother, I said, "If it's true, if Jordan really is dead, George and Lynn want him to be buried beside Larry and Daddy. Can we bury him in your plot below where you will be?" I knew her answer even before I asked.

It took an hour to make the phone calls and another hour to get ready for us to leave Tom and Donna home alone. When the phoning was over, I walked into the kitchen where Wayne had deposited our fruits and vegetables. Then I looked at the bags and didn't know what to do with the contents. I had no idea what would be required of us in the days to come, how long we would be gone, or what we would need to do. Wayne found me in the kitchen, walking around in circles. "What can I do to help you?" he asked.

"Bring the cooler from the garage," I said, still walking in a circle although the familiar question, *What can I do to help you?* did help me. "After that, stay with me wherever I am. If you don't, I'll just keep going in circles." I didn't know why we were taking the large cooler except that I seemed to taking the produce with us and some of it would do better on ice. It was unnecessary since I could have left them in the fridge, but I was doing it anyway.

When we were ready to pack the car, Tom told us to take his car. "It's better than your old car, Mom," he said, "and Dad can't take his company van." Grateful to be driving into the night without worrying about mechanical problems, we tossed our things into Tom's Corolla and kissed our two children good-bye. As we drove, stopping only to change drivers and make brief calls to George, we prayed. We prayed for a miracle. We prayed for grace.

I knew from experience that if the One didn't work the miracle I most wanted, for my little grandson to be born alive and healthy, there would be another miracle in its place. A miracle of Grace. As I faced the death of a beloved again, I knew, if it proved true, that Spirit would come to me and inhabit my broken spaces. Nothing would be required of me for this to happen, except that I open to the One in this hardest of all hard things.

Chapter 9

❀ ❀ ❀

As we drove through that night, I begged God to let me hold Jordan, to fill my ears with the sweet music of his crying. But if I could not have this, I wanted something else with all my heart. I wanted to celebrate my little grandson's life in all the ways available to me. I wanted to shout to the heavens that this baby's life and death had meaning. I wanted to know beyond doubt that Jordan would not be forgotten.

Sometime in the early morning hours, I dozed off while Wayne drove. Later, he told me that as we approached a bend in the road, he felt a deep peace come upon him. Then, as we rounded the bend, he saw a street sign. It said, *Jordan's Road.* He knew the One was speaking to him although he didn't know what the sign meant. He hoped it was the promise of a miracle, a sign that Jordan would be born alive. But whatever the outcome, he knew for certain now that Jordan's life was meant for peace.

I didn't sleep long and as we approached our destination, I realized that I had no idea how to hold my children in this experience. Whatever they might need from me in the hours and days to come, it would be something completely new to us. The death of an infant, whether by abortion, miscarriage, stillbirth or crib death, always seemed to me to be an unimaginable wound to the mother. I arrived at George's home then with no script for what might lie ahead. I knew only that I would hold my children and grandchildren in whatever way they needed to be held.

I learned later that Lynn arrived at the birthing center on Sunday feeling ready to apologize for being a worrywart. Laughing over the tricks pregnancy plays on expectant mothers, even skilled labor and delivery nurses, the attending nurse hooked Lynn up to a fetal monitor. Then the two nurses listened together for the reassuring sound of Jordan's heartbeat. When it was clear there was no sound, George was notified. Two sonograms, one by a doctor and another by an ultrasound specialist, confirmed the worst. Jordan had died in utero. By then, the silence of the birthing center had been pierced by a mother's frantic wailing and a father's heartrending efforts to hold his broken family together.

You imagine your child, as he is growing, in all sorts of situations. You imagine arriving at his graduation and seeing him sitting proudly with his classmates as they wait to receive their diplomas. You imagine him on a soccer field in some nearby town, coaching your grandchild through his or her first game. You imagine yourself being there to cheer both of them on. You do not imagine your child awaiting the birth of his stillborn son, and you do not imagine yourself arriving to help him through the experience. There are no road maps for something like this. And there isn't much to connect you to other human beings who have traveled this same path before you, either. It isn't the kind of thing people talk about around the dinner table. It isn't something they trade tips about over coffee break at work.

When Wayne and I pulled up to George and Lynn's house, it was about 3:30 in the morning. George came out to greet us, looking wan and tired but relieved to see us. I thought when I saw him that I always had been his "fix-it mommy." But this? I knew I couldn't fix this. He led us through the living room, where Kenny and Justice were sleeping on couches, and down the hallway to the stairs. "Do you want to see Lynn?" he asked.

"Does she want to see me?" I asked back. I wouldn't have faulted her if she wanted to block everyone out. George nodded that she did and led Wayne and me up the stairwell to their darkened bedroom. As I followed him, I prayed, "If Spirit ever is to flow through me, let it be now." When we reached the doorway, I made out Lynn's form on the right side of their bed and saw the outline of her belly. She was crying quietly and I went to kneel beside her. I put my hand on her and began to weep as well. George went to the other side of the bed. "It's okay," he said quietly, reaching over to comfort us both.

"Honey," I said, looking up at his dear face. "This is as not okay as it gets."

My son nodded.

Then I felt such tenderness for him that I added, "Maybe that's why we have men and women at a time like this. The men have to be strong, but the women are just going to weep." Lynn and I continued weeping and as my son held his wife, I heard him crying quietly, too.

I began to pray aloud then. I don't remember what I said. I just know I felt like a river of supplication for my children, especially for Lynn. And I prayed for Jordan. I asked the One to be present in a depth none of us had experienced before. I begged for strength for Lynn and comfort for George. I pleaded for them, asking that they be given a way to say yes to this hardest of all things, now that it was to be theirs forever.

When it was time to go, I told Lynn I loved her and followed Wayne into our granddaughter Amanda's room, to the beds we had occupied only two weeks before. Sometime after 5:00, I heard Lynn's parents arriving and from the voices below I could tell that Melissa, Lynn's only sibling, was with them. I knew Lynn's family and George would be at the hospital for Jordan's birth. I didn't know what would be needed from Wayne and me. George came to get us about 8:30, however. "We want you at the hospital with us," he said. "They are starting the drip to induce labor. Kenny will stay with Amanda and Justice. Bring your camera. We've decided we want pictures."

"So no heartbeat," I said.

"No heartbeat," he said.

This is it, then, I thought, accepting that there would not be the miracle I wanted most. Turning my heart to the One, I prayed, *Make us strong and help us stay in Grace.*

After a few quick calls to update our circle of prayer, Wayne and I left the house for the hospital. When we got there, Wayne let me out at the door to the birthing center while he parked the car. Lynn's mother, Lisa, was standing outside Lynn's room when I arrived, leaning against a wall. Tears streamed down her face. "I don't know how Lynn's going to get through this," Lisa said. "I'm afraid it's going to destroy her." I didn't know Lisa well, but I knew that I wanted to hug this tiny woman. I felt big and substantial as I reached over to hold her. I wanted to tell her that this would not destroy Lynn, that Lynn would say yes to Spirit and be filled over time with grace and gratitude fierce enough to hold all the grief and pain. But for now, I could only hug Lisa and cry with her.

When I saw Lynn, she looked sorrowful but composed. She was in bed hooked up to an IV drip and a machine that monitored the progress of her contractions. She explained they had begun inducing contractions already, but she had chosen medication to mask the birth pains and keep her dozing off and on throughout her labor. She didn't know how long the process would take.

My nephew Martin's song, "Save Me Now," played in the background. Lynn had been especially moved by it when she first heard the song at my father's funeral so Martin had made a tape of it for her. Now its plaintive words and melody cradled the room. "O Father who made me, take me, re-create me. O Father who loves me, hold me. O Jesus who conquered death and saved the world in the same breath, save me now..." I marveled at Lynn's openness, that she would invite both sides of her family to be part of this intimate and disturbing time. I wondered at how she had been given the wisdom to ask for and accept all the love she could find.

The birthing center itself was hushed as if it, too, were in mourning, holding its breath for this baby, the one that would never breathe, to be born. Lynn's room was large and had no difficulty accommodating all seven of us. Her favorite doctor promised to take a take a break, whenever the time came, and deliver Jordan himself.

During those first few hours, it felt as if we were preparing for a sacred dance. Seven people who hadn't practiced their parts beforehand now were being asked to perform a final dance created by an unseen choreographer. I was acutely aware of the differences among us. John and Lisa steeped in solid traditional American values; Wayne and I clinging to hippie vestiges from the sixties; George, Lynn and Melissa born in the seventies and raised in such different environments. I marveled then at the wisdom of the One. George and Lynn needed all of us to love them and to move together with them as if sharing one heart. The birthing center seemed aware of the upcoming dance as well. It held us tenderly and carefully, respectful of the dance and the way we would be changed before the last bow.

I had felt grateful to the staff for sending Lynn home the day before, for allowing her and George to prepare themselves for Jordan's birth, for giving their families time to arrive from such distances. But now my appreciation for the staff's enlightened methods grew. Then I remembered the four men in Wayne's family, working together in unity to release Vera's body into her death. And I thought that miracles do happen, that the peace of Spirit is visceral even in the most awful of human times.

As we waited for Jordan's birth, I found ways to ask Cara, Lynn's nurse, questions in private about what was ahead. She seemed exceptionally gifted in her profession and tender beyond words. With her help, I began to understand what George and Lynn would need and how I might help guide them. Sooner than expected, Lynn was fully dilated. One by one then, each of us gave her love and prayers for upholding.

Finding myself last in the room, alone with George and Lynn, I knew it was time to pray aloud. I asked Spirit again to pray through me and again, I was given words I could not have found by myself. Then George started the tape in the player again and Martin's lyrics flooded the birthing room. "O Father who made me, take me, re-create me. O Father who loves me, hold me..."

As the door swung shut behind me, my first thought was to update our prayer support. Wayne and I asked for a telephone, thinking we would be directed to a pay phone. Instead, we were given a vacant birthing room with the blessing of quiet and privacy. "It's time," I said as I called. "Lynn is giving birth right now. Stop whatever you're doing and pray."

Chapter 10

❀ ❀ ❀

It seemed only minutes before Cara was calling us back to Lynn's room. "The delivery went well," she said. Then she answered our silent question. "There's no sign of what went wrong. The baby is beautiful. He's perfect."

So it's the worst news to handle, I thought. *No miracle of healing. No last-minute change in the outcome. No little baby crying and kicking, but no life-threatening deformity either. No cord around his neck. No sign of trauma. Just a baby perfect in every detail except the one that most matters.*

When we went back into the room, Lynn was holding Jordan and sobbing. Melissa went to her and held her sister's head, whispering to her as tears streamed down both their faces. Pierced to my core as I watched them, I still thought, *What's the most natural thing to do when you're handed a newborn baby?*

Any mother knows you unwrap him from his blanket. You look at his little body and count his fingers and his toes. I remembered then my vow to be completely present in this experience, to celebrate my grandson's life in all the ways available to me, to shout to the heavens that this baby's life and death had meaning, and to never forget. With that, I went to Lynn and her mother, asking permission to unwrap the baby. Lynn nodded and held him out to me.

I knew from talking to Cara that Jordan's body would be soft and pliable, that his skin tone would not be like that of a live baby. I moved carefully as I unwrapped the blanket and was surprised to find him so pink. He was still spotted with blood from his birth and with the white cheesy substance that covers a newborn. My hands took on his musty smell. His little feet and hands were beautiful. I counted ten fingers and ten toes.

I continued looking over my grandson's body, up his chest and around his neck until finally I looked at his face. When my gaze reached it, though, I felt a gasp in my throat and hurried to stifle it. I had seen Jordan's face before. It was that of the dead infant in my early morning dream. "He has Amanda's eyes and forehead," I said quickly, not wanting Lynn to know I'd been startled. "His nose and mouth belong to Justice though."

Lynn, Lisa and Melissa began looking over the baby's body, too, and commenting on his resemblances. Then the photofest began. We passed Jordan around and took pictures of each of us holding him. Then we gave him back to Lynn and asked Cara to take photos of us around the two of them. And as we took pictures, we talked the way women do.

Jordan Peace Clifford was born into this world at 12:30 p.m. on Monday, April 10, 2000. Lynn said the birth was painless for her, although the medication made her vague on the details. George, normally talkative, was quiet, taking it all in. Then Lynn's friend, Anna, arrived with clothing for Jordan. Anna had shopped for just the right outfit and now brought a soft blue jumper, a blue beanie and a fuzzy blue blanket.

Lynn decided to have Jordan dressed for burial after the baby nurse cleaned him up from his birth. Lisa, Melissa and I left the room to give George and Lynn privacy while the nurse washed Jordan's body, weighed and measured it, and put on the clothing. While I waited in the hallway, I had a chance to ask Cara for further guidance. *Our family needs time with this,* I thought, *and we need ways to make it real.*

When we were called back into the room, the baby nurse told us that Jordan weighed five pounds, fourteen ounces, measured nineteen and a half inches, and appeared to be thirty-six weeks in gestation. He looked precious in his outfit and soon we went back to the photofest. I glanced away from Lynn for a moment and then turned just in time to see it. The miracle photo.

Lynn was holding Jordan and had slipped her right forefinger between his left thumb and forefinger. Framed now by the blue of his jumper and the white of her hospital gown, their joined hands spoke of an unending tenderness.

The gold locket from Amanda and Justice showed around Lynn's neck as well. If I caught the photo just so, I could catch the locket as well. "I want a picture of your hands," I told Lynn, "but I have to frame it just right." I took shots with both of our cameras and prayed one of them would be perfect.

Amanda, Justice and Kenny had accompanied Anna on her shopping trip. Now all three of them sat in the waiting room. I went to be with them and when I could take Kenny aside, I told him about Jordan's birth. I kept thinking that he needed a way to make this real for him. When I asked him if he wanted to see his baby nephew, Kenny grew pale, tears about to fall. "I don't know if I can," he said. His voice was desperate.

"It's better than you think," I said as gently as I could. "Clearly, it's your choice, but it's your only chance to get to know Jordan. Now while he's still in the hospital." I didn't know how long George and Lynn would decide to remain in the hospital or what would happen after they left. "I will help you if you choose to see him," I said. "And I truly believe you will be glad later if you do."

"Help me then," Kenny said, still holding back tears. It wasn't easy for him. It took several tries before he could enter Lynn's room. At one point, he took off down the hall, great sobs wracking his whole body. I thought then he might not be able to come back, but he did. And finally, he found courage to ease into the room and allow Baby Jordan to become real for him.

At some point, I learned that Amanda was asking to see her brother. Jordan was dressed in his blue outfit by then and snuggled in his mother's arms. *Amanda is eight. She's old enough to see her baby brother and she needs to make Jordan real for herself,* I thought. *She is asking because she knows that she needs to see him.* I went into the waiting room to talk with Amanda. Then I brought her request back to Lynn. "I think she needs to see him," I said, "but you decide." Lynn thought it over and nodded.

When Amanda was ushered into the room, she stood beside her mother and her tiny brother's body, watching them both with a grave countenance and a thoughtful mind. I could see the wheels turning as she studied Jordan, telling herself this was the baby for whom she never would play the big sister, the little brother who never would bug her, the sibling who never would joke with her and laugh at her stories. Someone asked Amanda if she wanted to touch Jordan and she shook her head. Standing beside him and watching was enough.

Minutes passed. Then Amanda indicated she was ready to go back to the waiting room. "What about Justice?" someone asked. I shook my head no. At five, Justice was too young and too attached to his mother to see her grieving in a hospital bed like this. He would not be able to know fully the source of her pain and might worry that she too was dying. *Still,* I thought, *Jordan is real for Amanda now. How do we make him real for Justice?*

Some understanding had passed between Lisa and me that afternoon about who would take what role in the delicate drama we were enacting. Not a lot was said, except for the most important thing. We both wanted George and Lynn to have everything they needed. Throughout that day and the days to follow, Lisa kept repeating the same phrases, "whatever Lynn needs" and "whatever Lynn wants." I saw her empty herself of her own desires and open herself up to be a pure vessel of love for her daughter.

Beyond our shared desire to serve our children, Lynn and I moved into the roles that fit each of us best. She thought about how we would get through the day. What we would eat and how the children would be clothed and cared for. I focused on logistics for the days ahead and how events could be structured so that George and Lynn would be given the best options possible. In all this, John cared for Lisa and Wayne cared for me.

By the end of the afternoon, it was clear that George and Lynn needed time alone. I knew from my talks with Cara that Lynn would be allowed to spend two days and two nights in the birthing center. Lynn's room included a bed chair for George. "We'll keep Jordan here for as long as you want," Cara told me. "George and Lynn can ask for him anytime they want and we will bring him to their room."

"How can you do that?" I asked, wondering how they planned to keep Jordan's body from deteriorating.

Cara smiled sadly. "We'll keep him on ice in the lab. You need to be ready for his body to be cold."

"How long can we hold him?" I asked. "Is there a time limit?"

Cara shook her head. "Not really," she said. "Usually people can hold their baby for as long as they need. Just let me know when Lynn and George are prepared to give Jordan up for the first time."

Later when they were ready to part with Jordan for a while, I told Cara I would carry him and follow her to the lab. It felt crucial to me that I do the grandmotherly things for him. I had only a few hours, a few days at best, to be his grandma in any physical sense of the word. Without making a nuisance of myself, I wanted that privilege.

As I walked down a new labyrinth of hospital corridors, this time with my grandson in my arms, I thought of the other hospital maze. Of the way I had listened with my whole heart on Vera's behalf, listened for the next thing. Cara and I walked in procession until we came to the laboratory door. Then she took Jordan from my arms.

Chapter 11

❀ ❀ ❀

My thoughts turned to Jordan's burial now. I knew Lynn would want her family to be with us. For this to be possible, she would need to be cleared to travel almost immediately, however. As her family had flown from the Midwest to San Francisco on nonrefundable round-trip tickets, time was of the essence. Lynn could stay in the hospital for a second day and night, but we would have to leave on Wednesday morning to drive south. This would give us tomorrow to make funeral arrangements and Wednesday to drive the fourteen hours home. If all of us were to attend Jordan's funeral, it would have to be held on Thursday morning.

I thought we could accomplish all this, but I doubted I would find much time for sleep. Before I left the hospital that night, I found an occasion to talk with Lynn in private. It seemed unfair to ask her questions like these only hours after giving birth, but I needed to know what was important to her. I wanted to learn, if I could, what she would choose if she could be the one planning the details. When I asked her, she looked dazed, however. I understood then that she had no way of understanding her options, of knowing the possibilities.

"If the doctor says it's okay and you feel you can travel on Wednesday, you could make the drive down to our house," I told her. "It's possible for us to have Jordan's service while your family is in California. I've talked to your mom about it and they want to come down to Orange County with you if that's what you want. For everything to work out though, the funeral has to be on Thursday. This doesn't give us much time, but I think we can manage it."

"We could do that?" she asked. "My folks could be with us?" She seemed both surprised and relieved.

"I think so." I smiled at her bewilderment. "If you want me to, I'll check on everything and decide for sure tonight."

"If my folks can be there, then that's what I want," she said.

A heavenly kindness hovered over Wayne and me as we went about our work. My sister Elizabeth and my friend Holly functioned as my eyes and ears at home. Father Richard, our friend and retired priest, worked on preparations for the service from his house. I began realizing that Wayne and I had rehearsed for this already. Although we didn't know it at the time, his mother's death and the celebration of her life prepared us to understand what was needed in our grandson's death and in the celebration of his life.

After Wayne and I had worked out the logistics, I talked things over with Lynn and George. We discussed details and encouraged by their responses, I moved to the hardest part. "It's unfortunate, but we have to decide about Jordan's body tonight," I said. "We can have him shipped to Orange County. It's expensive, but the cost isn't a factor in my mind. The big thing against having his body shipped is that we will have to give him up right away. The mortuary will send someone for him in the morning and we'll never be able to hold him again. We want you to have more time with Jordan, though. And it's legal for us to take his body with us in the car when Dad and I drive home."

For us, this was like asking someone to choose between a one-dollar and a hundred-dollar bill. There wasn't much to consider. I think we all knew my plan was unorthodox, but it wasn't as if we were aware of precedents. I'm told now that what we did was not merely unusual but that some people can't conceive of such a thing. I didn't find it strange, however. Strange would have been not to have the comfort of Jordan's body over the next three days. Strange would have been to give up my grandson's small body to strangers and to have him shipped off like a package, alone without family and without love.

Later Lynn asked me, "Where will we go after it's over? Will we all go to the Olive Garden for dinner?" That's what we had done after Vera's memorial service.

I wondered now if Lynn thought this was a family tradition. She seemed so earnest and so vulnerable. "If it's what you want, we will," I said, smiling at her.

It wasn't until after midnight, when I tried to get some sleep, that I realized I needed something for myself. There was something amiss for me in the energy of my birth family. My mother was holding me as she always did, serving as my best prayer warrior over the miles. My little sister had surprised me with the depth of her grief and the ferocity with which I felt her hovering over me. She seemed to be listening with every fiber of her being for the slightest hint of what I might need. Whenever I called her with a request, the word "anything" came out of her mouth before I even asked. I was almost ten years older than Elizabeth and I was used to holding her, not being held myself. Somehow in the events of Jordan's death, however, we had traded places and now she was holding me instead. My older siblings, though, were curiously absent.

My older brother, Will, was on a business trip and although I had put in a call to him through his wife, he had not returned it. I had talked to my older sister several times, but Helen seemed strangely distant. The last time we spoke, she said with sadness in her voice, "I think you've finally gone some place I can't go."

It wasn't that I questioned the love of my older siblings for me and it wasn't that I lacked emotional support. Elizabeth, in this experience, was enough for three siblings. It was just that I felt somehow incomplete without them. I knew Will would be at the funeral on Thursday morning, even if his wife couldn't reach him before he arrived home Wednesday night from his trip. But Helen hadn't said anything about flying out from the East Coast to be with us.

The night wore on and as I couldn't sleep, I got up to work on plans for the funeral. At one point, I passed through the kitchen and noticed the screen saver on Kenny's desktop computer. A single word in red capital letters tracked across it, an eerie tribute to our loss. The word was PEACE.

I began making lists of things to be done. Then I remembered the three-hour time difference between California and Pennsylvania and realized Helen would be up now, getting ready for work. I decided to call again. When I reached her, we chatted for a few moments before I said, "I'm calling to say that I know you've been distant from me over Jordan's death."

Helen said, "Yes."

"I don't know why," I went on, "and I forgive you, whatever the reason. But you aren't holding me the way you usually do. I miss you and I just want you to know Thursday won't be the same without you. You won't be there to hold George and Lynn in that warm embrace of yours. And when Elizabeth and I sing "Kingdom Citizen," you won't be there to sing with us." I started crying then and Helen cried, too. "I know how much you love me," I went on, "and I accept the way you are with me right now. But I miss you."

"I would give anything to be there with you," Helen said through her tears.

"Then why aren't you coming?" I asked, relieved to give voice to the one missing ingredient for Thursday's celebration. "George and Lynn keep asking if you're coming and I don't know how to answer."

By the time I hung up the phone, my big sister was making arrangements to get time off work and fly out on Wednesday. She would be at my house when I arrived. I learned she was coping with intense emotional pain in her own life at the moment and didn't know how to be enough for me in mine. As we talked, however, she understood I didn't need one particular thing or another from her. I just needed her to come.

It will be real for Helen now, I told myself as I went back to bed, *and I know I'll hear from Will soon. For the rest of my life when I look back on Thursday, I will know that my three siblings were there with me on that singular day.* I closed my eyes then, thinking about my Berry family and praying the One would keep all eight of us in the eternal embrace.

Chapter 12

❀ ❀ ❀

I slept for a few hours and awoke to a day seemingly orchestrated from above. It was as if some kindly unseen secretary had made all my Tuesday appointments for me. George arrived early with news about the hospital nursery. He said it was just down the hall from their birthing room and vacant at the moment. "You need to be there with me, Mom," he said. "I sat in the rocker last night and held Jordan there. It's so much better than the birthing room!"

When I arrived at the birthing center, it was as quiet as the day before. I marveled at how the building seemed to exist only for us. George took me to the nursery and Lynn's nurse brought Jordan's body to us. Then I sat in the rocking chair, among the cribs and bassinets, and held my grandson, whispering to him as I studied his little face. Although he was cold now and had been out of the womb for almost a day, his body still was soft and pliable, his skin a rosy color.

How sad that death is so removed from us in our culture,
I thought. We all die. It's the one thing we can count on
when we're born. Yet most people in this country seem to
fear dead bodies. Maybe it's because they don't know what
to expect. Death was not removed from me growing up in
Honduras. Maybe that's partly why I wasn't afraid to hold
my grandson and rock him. But mostly, it had to do with
love. It's hard to fear something you love.

It was wonder-filled for me to be with Jordan in the
setting of a nursery. I wanted to have as much time there
with him as possible. I wanted to rock him and sing him
all the songs I would have sung if he had lived. But other
arrangements needed to be made first. I left the hospital
soon to meet up with Wayne and drive around to the two
mortuaries in the area.

Our plan was to look at infant caskets and ask questions
about how to transport Jordan's body. Lynn and I had
talked about the casket and found we both wanted the same
thing. Like boyish baby clothes for a little boy, we wanted
something that couldn't be interpreted as anything else. We
wanted something that said clearly, *Dearly Beloved Baby
Boy.*

The staff at the first mortuary were not helpful and
the two basic infant caskets available were not right for
Jordan either. The staff at the second were wonderfully
kind, helpful and tender, giving of their time. When they
offered anything they could do to help, free of charge, I
asked, "How do you make any money then?"

"When it's a baby, even those of us who deal with death all the time feel a special sorrow," the mortician said. "Advising you on this isn't something I would want money for." He went on to explain that because infant deaths weren't common, they kept only a few basic casket models in stock. "It's too bad we're not in a metropolitan area," he said, "where you would have better choices."

"Oh, but I live between San Diego and Los Angeles!" I said with excitement. "My sister and my friend can look for me." Elizabeth and Holly both were mothers and would know, just as Lynn and I had, what was right for Jordan. Certainly, there would be more choices for Holly, who lived near San Diego, and Elizabeth, who lived near Los Angeles.

I went on then to ask the mortician if he would explain to me, as simply as possible, what was needed to keep Jordan's body preserved until we could place him in his casket. I soon understood the only items required were a large cooler, something we already had, and thick plastic to cradle his body as he rested on a bed of ice.

Later that day, we had a dedication service for Jordan in the hospital chapel. We processed down the same halls I had walked the day before with Jordan in my arms. This time Lynn carried him, supported by her husband on one side and her father on the other. When we reached the chapel, we sat in the first rows. Gathered there were our little family and some of Lynn's friends. The priest welcomed us and said a prayer of dedication. Then I read from Psalm 139, using *The Living Bible* translation my parents had given George on his tenth birthday. My voice stayed strong as I read, and I felt the gladness of every word.

O Lord, you have examined my heart and know everything about me. You know when I sit or stand. When far away you know my every thought. You chart the path ahead of me, and tell me where to stop and rest. Every moment, you know where I am. You know what I am going to say before I even say it. You both precede and follow me, and place your hand of blessing on my head.

This is too glorious, too wonderful to believe. I can never be lost to your Spirit. If I go up to heaven, you are there; if I go down to the place of the dead, you are there. If I ride the morning winds to the farthest oceans, even there your hand will guide me, your strength will support me. If I try to hide in the darkness, the night becomes light around me. For even darkness cannot hide from God; to you the night shines as bright as day. Darkness and light are both alike to you.

You made all the delicate, inner parts of my body, and knit them together in my mother's womb. Thank you for making me so wonderfully complex. It is amazing to think about. Your workmanship is marvelous, and how well I know it. You were there while I was being formed in utter seclusion. You saw me before I was born and scheduled each day of my life before I began to breathe. Every day was recorded in your book.

How precious it is, Lord, to realize that you are thinking about me constantly. I can't even count how many times a day your thoughts turn towards me. And when I awaken in the morning, you are still thinking of me. Search me, O God, and know my heart; test my thoughts. Point out anything you find in me that makes you sad, and lead me along the path of everlasting life.

When I finished reading, I thought of the mantra Lynn now repeated to herself. "I have three children. Two of them live on this earth and one of them lives in heaven." Jordan Peace Clifford was alive. Although his experience of earthly things was limited to thirty-six weeks hidden in his mother's womb, he lived on. *Jordan was formed by the one loving force that cradles all life,* I told myself. *And now my little grandson has stepped into "the next room," where he is part of the cosmic dance forever.*

After the priest baptized Jordan, he closed with a prayer. In the quiet that followed, I knew I wanted to sing. *My family will understand, although other people might think I'm crazy,* I told myself, all the while knowing that I didn't care. Since the beginning of George's phone call on the lawn of our home two days before, I had lost all caring for convention or what anybody outside my family thought of me. This time simply was too important to expend a millisecond worrying about appearances.

I sang "In Your Time" first. The tender words and melody caressed the small chapel as my voice stayed true.

In Your time, in Your time,
You make all things beautiful in Your time.
Oh, please show me every day,
As You're teaching me Your way,
That You do just what You say in Your time.

> **In Your time, in Your time,**
> **You make all things beautiful in Your time.**
> **Oh, my life to You I bring,**
> **May each song I have to sing,**
> **Be to You a lovely thing in Your time.**

When I finished, the moment seemed to want more song so I moved on to my lullaby. I had written it for Kenny shortly after his birth. Now I placed my hands on George and Lynn seated in front of me and holding Jordan. Then I sang again, my voice still strong.

> **Jordan, Jordan, the One has made you,**
> **Little vessel for this love.**
> **Jordan, Jordan, the One has blessed you,**
> **Sent you angels from above.**

> **Jordan, Jordan, little boy,**
> **Jordan, Jordan, little joy.**
> **The One has made you,**
> **The One has blessed you,**
> **Little vessel for this love.**

I felt a warming sense of completion when I finished. Jordan had been dedicated, baptized and blessed. And it was good.

Lisa put her arms around me later to thank me, both for the reading and the songs. I was happy to know that she had understood and not found my actions intrusive. I was delighted to learn soon after as well that Holly had located a casket. "It's what I would choose if Jordan was my baby," she said. I knew I trusted Holly's sense of it, but I didn't yet know how important that little blue-and-white checkered gingham-covered casket would become to us.

Lynn wanted a picture of Jordan for the altar at the funeral service as well. My best hope was the "miracle photo" of Lynn and Jordan's hands. If it appeared on film the way it had formed in my mind, it would be perfect. I took the film for instant development that afternoon and the shop did a masterful job. The colors were bright and true. When I saw the "hands" pictures, I gave out a shout of joy. One of them was framed perfectly, reflecting exactly what I had seen the day before. Most of the other photos were hard to look at, however. I shuffled and reshuffled the prints until I finally selected some to put in an album right away for George and Lynn. From these, I chose four to make a separate collage for the altar.

When Wayne and I arrived back at the hospital, I gave Lynn the photo album. "Most of the pictures are hard to look at," I told her. "I think it's best if you wait until later to see those. The easiest ones are in this album I made up for you, and here are four others I think we can display on Thursday."

Lynn studied me for a moment, then nodded. She paged through the photo album sadly and then pointed to one of her holding Jordan, a heart-wrenching look of pain and longing on her face. "I want this one for Thursday, too," she said. "I want everybody to be able to really see him.

What can I do, though, because I don't want to part with it before then?"

It was a beautiful picture. I hadn't known she would want to be so vulnerable, though. "Keep it with you and I will get it from you just before the service," I said. "I'll put it on the altar in a frame by itself."

I left on other errands after that and returned to the hospital late in the afternoon to rock Jordan again. Lynn's parents were with her in the birthing room. At first I was alone with Jordan, but one by one, Wayne, Kenny and George filtered in. Tears streamed down my face and fell on his blue blanket as I sang to my grandson again. I sang my Spirit songs, my silly songs and my tender songs. And as I sang, my heart ached and ached for all the singing Jordan and I never would do together in our bodies again.

When I sang him "The Moon Song," I thought that from then on, it forever would be for him.

> **I see the moon, the moon sees me,**
> **The moon sees the one that I want to see.**
> **God bless the moon and God bless me,**
> **And God bless the one that I want to see.**
>
> **I do believe that God above,**
> **Created you and me to love.**
> **He picked you out from all the rest,**
> **Because he knew I'd love you best.**

These were sacred moments for us, especially since we knew these songs and this way of being together so well. Soon my songfest with Jordan turned into a photofest with all of us. All four Berry-Cliffords took turns holding him in the rocker and having our pictures taken, tears streaming down our faces. Later after my guys left, I sat with Jordan alone, again rocking him and wondering at how heavy his small body felt in my arms. I tried to imagine what type of baby he would have been and what his little personality might have been like. All I could think was that he would have been tough and tender like his older brother.

"I'll get to know you, sweetheart," I told him. "Someday soon, I'll step into the next room and you'll be there already. Look for me! I'm a grandma so it won't be too long before it's my turn." I smiled at myself then because I knew Jordan was living now where there was no time and for him, I already was beside him in eternity. Our human bodies were sitting in the hospital nursery. One big soft pillowy body rocked a small fragile one. But our spirits were equals already, united forever in that great heavenly dance.

Chapter 13

❀ ❀ ❀

Wayne and I left George and Lynn's house early on Wednesday morning. We stopped for ice, filling our beach cooler with it, before driving on to the hospital. I wasn't sure what should happen next. I only knew I wasn't going to roll the cooler down the hospital halls. Wayne left me off at the door to the birthing center and I went inside to ask Lynn's nurses for help. Someone called the administrator and she came right away. Margaret was a sympathetic woman, comfortable being in charge. For all she let me know, every parent and grandparent handled their stillborn baby's body this way. She asked if I had heavy enough plastic. When I said I wasn't sure, she found a sturdy hospital plastic for me.

"Is it all right to leave his little blanket around him?" I asked. "It's kind of thick."

"How far are you traveling?" she asked in return. I told her fourteen hours and she inquired further. "You'll place him in his casket tonight?"

I nodded. The blue-and-white gingham-covered casket would be waiting for us at home, upstairs in our bedroom.

"Then he'll be fine," she said with approval. "Just keep him in his blanket and make a nest of the plastic between his body and the ice. You won't have a problem."

"How do I get him?" I asked, wishing we had worked this out beforehand and wondering if Lynn and George needed to see Jordan one more time.

"I will bring Jordan to you," Margaret said. Then she added, as if reading my mind. "Do George and Lynn want to see him before he goes?"

"I'll ask them," I said, and went to find out. They did, so Margaret brought Jordan into their room where Wayne joined us. As she hovered over Lynn, helping her say good-bye to Jordan's body, I thought again of how gifted the hospital staff was with their gentle skills.

Finally, Margaret cradled Jordan and motioned for Wayne and me to follow. It took a moment to realize that she was treating us the same way she treated couples who had given birth to live babies. She walked us to the front door, stayed with me while Wayne brought the car around, watched me slide into the passenger's seat, handed me my grandbaby, said sweet things about all three of us, and wished us well for the long trip home.

As we pulled out of the sunny parking lot, I noticed a shady spot under a tree, across the street and away from traffic. "Over there," I said to Wayne. "Pull over there." Wayne parked the car under the tree and came around to take Jordan from me. I got out, opened the door behind me, and fitted the plastic over the ice in the cooler. Then Wayne gave Jordan back to me. I held him for a moment, kissed his forehead, and placed him tenderly in his plastic cocoon. "Ride well, sweet boy," I told him as I closed the cooler.

I sang on the ride home, and we talked a lot. I was surprised to find we still could laugh over silly stuff. As we drove, I contemplated Lynn and the gift she had given me in trusting us to take Jordan's body home. In this deeply loving act, she had allowed me to watch over my grandson with the same vigilant care I would have used if he were alive. Her infant's body was my responsibility now. It would be mine until we arrived at the cemetery the next morning. I intended to honor my daughter-in-law with every breath I took and I thanked her, perhaps more than she could ever know, for the privilege she had given me.

It was on the drive home that Wayne finally told me of the peace he had experienced as he drove through the night praying for Jordan's safe delivery. He told me about rounding the bend and encountering the sign that said, *Jordan's Road*. "I didn't know what it meant," he told me, "and that's why I didn't say anything to you about it before. I thought maybe it meant Jordan would be born alive, though. I felt so much peace about him when I saw the sign. In any case, it was something very special and I'm glad I was given that experience."

As I listened to Wayne speak, something new began forming within me. I remained quiet, trying to hear and to honor the creative process. It was something about *Jordan's Road*. A familiar energy arising from my solar plexus began moving up toward my head. "Jordan's Road," I said finally. "It's the book the One has been speaking to me about for a long time." And for the rest of the trip, I felt bursts of joy at finally knowing this.

I talked to Elizabeth while we were on the road, telling her we'd get there before midnight and asking her to have the house quiet, cleared of other people before we arrived. "I want you and Helen to be downstairs when we arrive and then to go upstairs with me after I take Jordan up to our room," I told her. My sisters would be waiting for us when we got home.

I had a long night ahead of me and I doubted I would go to bed. There was too much to be done before the funeral. We needed to leave our home for the cemetery at 8:00 in the morning and I wanted to be ready. Not only did I want to spend time with my sisters and decide how to place Jordan in his coffin, I needed to find the best way to make Jordan real for our son Tom who had stayed home with Donna and missed all the family bonding time with Jordan up north. If that could be accomplished tonight, it would leave only Donna and Justice who hadn't made a connection with our baby. I had been listening for wisdom on how to help them, but nothing had come to me yet. Justice would never see Jordan. Once Jordan was in his coffin and I shut the lid, it wouldn't be opened again. I didn't know how to anticipate

Donna's needs upon our arrival so I'd asked for her to go to bed at her usual time.

Elizabeth and Helen rushed out of the house as soon as we pulled into the driveway. I wanted to carry Jordan into the house in my arms, the same way Margaret had given him to me at the hospital. But I wanted him to be cradled in a larger blanket. Although I knew his little body well by now, I didn't know how my sisters would respond. I wanted Jordan to feel warmer and more substantial to them when I offered to let them hold him. I got out of the car and asked them to wait for us inside. They scurried off like chastened children. I wanted to laugh and cry at the same time as I watched them. I waited a couple of minutes and then headed inside to retrieve the blue afghan I needed.

What I saw when I walked past the living room made me want to drop to my knees. Helen and Elizabeth were huddled on the couch, hands intertwined, heads bowed in prayer. I recognized what they were feeling because I, too, was gripped by the same fervent desire. I wanted to listen so intently for what was right for Lynn that even the pores on my skin would join in the listening. Looking at my sisters now, I knew they felt the need for that same kind of listening on my behalf. I recognized this then as a deep love intimately connected to Source. An unending love arising from the One within us. In that moment, I felt this holy love from my sisters so deeply that I wanted to cry.

I found the blue afghan and took it back to the car. Wayne held the blanket for me as I lifted Jordan's body from the cooler. I wrapped Jordan in it and then Wayne escorted me back into the house. As I passed my sisters, I indicated for them to follow me up the stairs. When the door was shut behind us, I handed the baby to Elizabeth. She gave a groan as I put Jordan into her arms and then said aloud to herself, "I can do this."

I watched her from my bed as she sat in the rocking chair and let go of her fear, thus allowing Jordan to become real for her. A remarkable change came over her. As she held Jordan's body and looked into his little face, Elizabeth began cuddling him, patting his bottom while rocking the chair gently back and forth. I knew then from watching her that she was making a love connection with her great-nephew and that she would not have had it any other way.

Helen's turn was next, but she couldn't hold him. All she could do was to sob, and that was enough. I recognized both the tenderness and the anguish in my older sister's voice and although I felt holding Jordan would be healing for her, I knew this was her journey and not mine.

I sat with my sisters later, talking about the trip and my time away, getting myself ready for the inevitable task of placing Jordan's body in his coffin. The casket itself was more than I could have hoped for. Truly, Holly had been my angel in selecting something so perfect. It was shaped like a traditional coffin, but tinier than I could have imagined. Only twenty-one inches long, it looked like a bed for a lovable doll.

The blue-and-white checks of gingham were complemented with white lace and blue ribbon trim. The gingham material covered both the inside and the outside of the box, all of it padded underneath with cotton batting. This made the casket soft to the touch, both inside and out. The manufacturer also had provided a sturdy outer shell. One that could be sealed, top and bottom, over the coffin to strengthen and protect it after it was lowered into the ground.

Finally, I turned my attention to Tom. I asked my sisters to wait in the bedroom while I went downstairs to knock on his door. I was glad he had stayed in his room while we arrived and from the sound of it now when I got to his door, Tom was on his knees praying up a storm. When I called to ask if he wanted to come up, he called back that he would come up as soon as he could.

Tom was composed when he entered our upstairs bedroom. Again, it was my privilege to watch my little grandson become real for another member of our family. Tom held Jordan tenderly, asked questions about him, and kissed his small forehead. He seemed in no hurry, simply wanting to stay in the grace of the moment. I knew I wanted the same thing for Donna who was fifteen, but I hadn't prepared her for it. And I was too exhausted to understand how I could awaken her at this late hour and have it be right for her. Instead, I said a prayer of thanksgiving that Tom had been able to hold Jordan and asked that I might be given strength and patience for the long night ahead.

Psalm 30 says that joy comes in the morning. When I told Helen and Elizabeth I was ready to be alone with Jordan, I knew the gifts of Spirit would be mine throughout the night. I knew we would work our way patiently toward the joy of the next morning. Wayne and I already had agreed that he would sleep in his office. And although he wasn't happy to know I might not sleep at all, he found a way to release his concern for my health and well-being.

When I finally was alone in our bedroom, the tasks before me became clear although my physical ability to accomplish them did not. I knew only that I was deeply exhausted and that Spirit would carry me. Wayne and my sisters had offered strenuously to help me, but I was too tired to explain anything to anyone. What I needed most was quiet to hear the next thing. And when that was accomplished, I needed unhurried time to listen for the next thing after that.

My checklist, if I'd had the mental wherewithal to make one, would have looked like this:

1. Decide how to arrange Jordan in his casket.

2. Organize the pieces of the jigsaw puzzle that are my plans for the funeral service.

3. Make the display for the altar.

4. Check all the purchases by Elizabeth and Holly to make sure everything is ready.

5. Make a final checklist for tomorrow morning.

6. Review the order of service Father Rob printed out.

7. Finalize and type out the readings, hymns and worship songs.

8. Write out the words you want to say at the cemetery because you'll be too tired to speak off the cuff.

It was 4:30 in the morning when I finally sat down at my computer. *I have the most important words of my life to write in the least amount of time,* I thought. Then I wanted to throw up. Finally, I began typing without pausing for thought. The One seemed to flow through my fingertips then. Words of thanksgiving came to my lips as my fingers moved. I soon finished and clicked the *print* icon.

After this, I arranged Jordan's body in his casket along with the mementos we had chosen to accompany him. Then I blessed him and closed the lid.

Chapter 14

※ ※ ※

"Surely goodness and mercy shall follow me all the days of my life." The words of Psalm 23 were ours the day of Jordan's funeral. It was the best kind of California day, not too cold and not too hot. Wayne helped me put Jordan's tiny checkered casket into its white shell and snap the latches tight. Then he took the casket to the back seat of the car, placing it where our cooler had been the day before.

I felt completely drained as we drove to Orange County. Knowing I had nothing more of myself to give, I simply trusted the One to sustain me and energize me until the celebration was over and we were safely at the restaurant. I wondered about the rest of my family and Lynn's family. How were they? I prayed for all of us to be sustained by Grace over the next few hours.

Problems with no ready solutions presented themselves as soon as we reached our family gravesite. Primary among them was that the sun would be moving over the course of the next few hours and there would be no way to keep everyone shaded all the time. *Just remember from the get-go,* I told myself, *this funeral celebration is going to be perfectly imperfect. Choose not to be concerned about those parts over which you have no control.*

As I requested, a large green canopy had been set up some distance from the shade tree near our family plots. I found a place beneath our tree to set Jordan's casket, glad to see that, in its white shell, it looked innocuous enough not to be noticed. Wayne and I selected a place under the canopy for the altar and set up small utility table. Then I draped a white crocheted tablecloth over it and arranged the components of the altar. In front of it, I put two little green chairs to remind me of Amanda and Justice. On one chair, I placed a basket of pens and notepaper and on the other, a basket of nametags.

Water, pretzels and blankets went in the center of the semicircled chairs. These were for the children if needed. Above them, baby-blue balloons engraved with the words "It's a boy!" floated under the canopy. To the left of the altar, we placed a small podium if anyone needed it and to the right, chairs for Martin and his wife as they led the music. Next to these chairs, I positioned a low wicker table. Jordan's casket would rest there after everyone had gathered, beside a special chair for Lynn. George would be seated next to her.

I knew Wayne and I needed to sit near the podium. Beyond that, I soon realized there would be no way to control the seating. There were not enough chairs for everyone as the cemetery already had set up for other services in other parts of the park. The kids could sit on blankets and adults who had beach chairs could get them out of their cars.

As the morning progressed, the list of things I needed to give up kept growing. It was like packing as carefully as you can for the ocean cruise of your life, then finding after the ship sails that you haven't anticipated everything. In a situation like this, there is only one good solution. Do what you can, then relax and enjoy the ride!

The flowers began arriving even before the people. The first to arrive were from George's military service, the Coast Guard, and then, to my delight, the flowers kept coming. It was not to my delight, however, when front row seats began filling up not with people we knew personally but with local representatives of the military that our family didn't know. *Like it or don't like it,* I told myself. *No matter, as long as you welcome whoever, whatever comes.*

George, Lynn and the kids arrived with the last group of guests. Lynn seemed dazed but composed as she was helped to her chair. Even in her silence, she was the picture of grief. I breathed a prayer of thanksgiving that her mother and father were seated right behind her. When everyone had gathered, I asked the kids to sit on blankets in the center.

Now that everyone was seated, Jordan's casket was conspicuously missing and I still had no plan for bringing it into the circle. Then inspiration hit. It was a tiny little casket and two little people could carry it. Perhaps this was part of the way for Jordan to become real for Justice. Amanda and Justice were seated with the other children already in the center of the canopy. I bent down and asked them to come with me. After that, we walked to the tree and knelt beside it. I explained Jordan's body was in the white box and asked if they wanted to help me by carrying it. Both were delighted so I unlatched the shell, separating the top from the bottom. Then I explained how Jordan's body had been placed inside his blue-and-white checkered casket and where his head and feet lay.

Amanda and Justice picked up the casket carefully with faces of utmost concentration. I followed them, ready to help if they stumbled, but they proudly carried their baby brother's casket into the circle with no need for help. After they placed the gingham coffin on the low table next to their mother, Amanda went back to sit with her friends, a smile of satisfaction on her face. Justice went to sit on his mother's lap. His self-appointed task for the rest of the service was that of comforter. He moved back and forth among the members of his family, patting and holding the one who seemed most in need of his ministrations. And in between all that activity, he kept trying to open the little casket. He knew, and the One knew, that he needed to see inside it.

Behind the altar now, Father Rob and his wife, Deacon Elaine, stood in the bright sun, their white robes falling around them. I hoped they would bend their liturgical rules enough to move into the shade in front of the altar when necessary. Another specific beyond my control.

"This is a celebration of Jordan's life," I said as I opened the service. "He lived cuddled up inside his mother for thirty-six weeks. We are so glad he came to be with us for that short time and we are very sad he could not stay with us longer. We are going to sit here, be family together, take our time to remember Jordan, and tell him that we will always love him. Jordan is unique. There will never be another person on this earth exactly like him. Jordan is irreplaceable and his short life is cause for celebration. It's kind of like a birthday and a good-bye party all rolled into one. Get comfortable. Kids, if you get hungry or thirsty, there is water and pretzels for you."

I went on to introduce everyone in the circle. It seemed to me that as many as sixty people were gathered. When all had been named and their relationship to our family explained, I moved on to what I had written. "Not too long ago, I was introduced to the concept that if it's worth doing, it's worth doing badly," I said. "I thought this was wonderful because it gave me permission to try things I wasn't good at. When I shared it with Wayne, though, he made it even better for me. He said, 'If it's worth doing, it's worth doing.'

"I want to tell you that of all the things I've done in my life, this celebration for our baby Jordan's life feels the most worth doing. You're looking at a sleepless woman. And I'm not the only sleepless person here today. I did my best to communicate the details of the service over the phone to all the wonderful people here who were helping me. I feel truly blessed at how everything has come together. You'll notice a lot of goofs along the way though, but that will only make it all the more real."

Days later when I watched the video of this part of the service, I observed myself as if the woman on the screen was a stranger. I looked at her tired, drawn face, and my heart filled with compassion for her. I knew that she was doing the humblest thing she had ever done and I knew that every fiber of her being wanted to be right in that very spot, at that very moment, saying those very words. I knew that if this birthday-and-good-bye party for her grandson had been written as a book, she would have wanted to recite every line, even the punctuation. I knew this was her gift to her children and that she wanted to serve them well. I watched her smile at the little kids, and move her round body as she talked, and I loved the look of her and the comfort of her. I thought she resembled a strong peasant woman from old European stock.

We began the service with short worship songs that could be sung easily, even if you had never heard them before. There have been many worship songs in our family's history, but I tried to pick those that could be sung without pause as we moved from one to the next. I wanted our singing to be like pouring water from one bowl to another, to another. And I wanted it to be as beautiful as it could be.

Lynn sat across from me as we sang, overcome with grief. She alternately patted Jordan's coffin and looked through the small photo album of his pictures. The importance of the gingham-covered casket began to unfold for me then. It was soft and huggable. Lynn would not be able to hold her baby, but she could hug, stroke and hold his coffin.

George and Lynn asked for a long time of singing, and they got it. It began with George's favorite worship song. "You are my hiding place. You always fill my heart with songs of deliverance. Whenever I am afraid, I will trust in you..." Although Martin didn't know every song I'd chosen, he played along on his guitar as we moved from one to the other. We worked together this way in a slightly confused manner, either he or I starting a song, depending on who seemed most ready.

After our singing, Father Rob began the Episcopal liturgy by saying the traditional "The Lord be with you." The congregation then responded, "And also with you." Later when it was time for Lynn to read, she seemed ready to do so. The passage was written by Leonard Clark and given to her at the birthing center the morning she learned Jordan had died. Lynn had asked me to adapt some of the lines so it would fit Jordan better. I gave it a new title as well. Now the words were displayed on the altar next to the photographs from Jordan's birth.

To Jordan from Your Mother

I carried you in hope, the long nine months of my term, remembered that close hour when we made you,

often felt you kick and move as slowly you grew within me, wondered what you would look like when your wet head emerged, and at what glad moment I should hear your birth cry. I welcomed you with all you needed of warmth and food; we had a home waiting for you.

After my strong laboring, sweat cold on my limbs, my cries merging with the spring air, you came. You did not cry. You did not breathe. They will say that you did not live, register you as stillborn. But you lived for me all that time in the dark chamber of my womb, and when I think of you now, perfect in your little death, I know that for me you are born still.

I shall carry you with me forever, my child; you were always mine, you are mine now. Death and life are the same mysteries.

Lynn cried softly as she read these words, but did not stop reading. When she was finished, Martin began singing "Save Me Now" with its familiar words. "O Father who made me, take me, re-create me. O Father who loves me, hold me..." Days later as I watched the scene from the vantage point of the camera, one small detail broke my heart. The camera caught Kenny's head in the foreground as he lost his composure. Then two small arms appeared to caress his head. Justice, the comforter, was present. Soon he rested his head on his uncle's head and waited for Uncle Kenny to scoop him up into his arms. One nephew was gone, and the other was on double duty.

Chapter 15

❀ ❀ ❀

A prayer formed within me as I stepped to the podium to begin our sharing time. I didn't know if the words I'd written in the early morning still would make sense. Then I began reading from the heart.

When Wayne and I were traveling to Eureka on Sunday, trying desperately to get there as quickly as possible, I fell asleep for a while. Wayne told me later about something that happened to him during this time. He was driving and praying and crying out when suddenly he felt a sense of deep peace. Then the car turned a bend in the road and he saw a sign straight ahead of him. It said, Jordan's Road.

I want to tell you what Jordan's Road has come to mean to me. If I could talk to the One right now face to face, I can't think of any reason for Jordan's death

that would be good enough. But the strange thing to me is that in the fact of Jordan's death, Grace to me is good enough. To me Jordan's Road is a choice to take the road less traveled. It is a choice to say yes to the One and follow the hard road that leads to the experience of overwhelming grace, to the peace that is not based in circumstances and that passes all understanding.

Our Baby Jordan is dead. He lives in the next room, but he is not here with us on this earth. There are so many things that I will never be able to do with him. No rocking him, no singing to him, not the marvelous pleasure of sleeping on the couch with his warm little body cuddled up on my tummy. No hugs and kisses. No stories. No sleepovers in the living room under the big tent with his sister and brother and his cousins and friends. The list goes on and on.

This little boy that I have come to love so much is dancing with the angels in heaven right now, but I can only imagine it. I am not a part of it until I, too, am allowed to step into the next room and join the dance. But Baby Jordan came to give us gifts. All of us who love him and whose hearts have been broken by his death have a choice. We can close down a part of ourselves to wall off the pain and protect ourselves from further pain. Or we can open ourselves up to this little baby and to the gifts his life and death have given us.

We can travel Jordan's Road. We can even embrace it. We can allow the suffering of this hardest of all gifts to deepen us and form the character of Christ in us.

We can let it soften us and make us more tender with each other and with ourselves. We can stop trying to be perfect and do things just because they are worth doing. We can beg the One to teach us what really matters and stop sweating the small stuff.

We can live a life of tremendous joy on Jordan's Road because we can stop being afraid of life, and death, and start loving the fact that we can get up in the morning and breathe air and touch our toes. At least some of us can touch our toes. We can kiss our loved ones and go about another day of living in gratitude. This is Jordan's Road. The Bible says that when the thing we fear most comes upon us, the One is on the other side of that experience. The thing we fear most has come upon us this week, but if we allow it, the One will come to us in a way that was not possible before Jordan's Road.

After my words and those of personal sharing from others, my sisters and I ended this time by singing "Kingdom Citizen." We sang it without accompaniment, except for tambourine on the chorus. When the last verse says, "How I love you, brother," we changed it just as we had for our father. This time we sang, "How I love you, little one."

The traditional break for passing the peace that precedes the Episcopal celebration of the Eucharist arrived and everyone needed to stretch. Then Eucharist began with The Great Thanksgiving and proceeded in an unerring march through the marvelous cadences of its sacred words. Few things in the world were quite as comforting to me as the Eucharist. The tenderness of so many people, young and old, coming to the altar for something they could not manufacture on their own always moved me to tears.

When the liturgy was over, Father Rob and Deacon Elaine administered the bread and the wine to us as we sat in our places. As the elements were passed, my sisters and I sang Jodi Page's incomparable communion song, "Please Break This Bread."

The most fun part of the service was still to come, however. "Jordan's life is very important to us," I told them. "Now that he is in heaven, we have a lot more love in our lives. We love Jordan now and it makes us love each other more. It makes us think about how special each of us is and how neat it is that we were made to do cool stuff. One of the cool things we can do is to sing and have fun. If Jordan could be here with us now, he would love to sit on his mommy's lap and laugh with us. One of the most fun songs is the one about the butterfly. You kids all know it and, grown-ups, if you know it you can sing and help us too."

The "Butterfly Song" written by Brian Howard has wonderful motions and everybody loves doing them because it's so easy to ham it up. The song begins with, "If I were a butterfly, I'd thank you, Lord, for giving me wings..." and moves on to other animals like the "fuzzy wuzzy bear" and the "octopus."

After we sang a few songs, I moved us on to the balloon ceremony. "See the balloons up there," I said, motioning for help to get them down. "Take one and hold it real tight in your hand. Don't let it go until I tell you. We are going to give a cheer for Baby Jordan and then let our balloons float up into the sky. That way, we're telling Baby Jordan how much we love him. We're going to go out from under the canopy to do it, but first we have to practice.

"I'm going to say, 'Hip, hip' and then I want you to shout, 'Hurray!' all together. We are going to do this three times, but on the last time, after I say 'Hip, hip,' you are going to yell 'Baby Jordan' at the top of your lungs. And when we do it for real, not right now because we are just practicing, I want you to let your balloons go all at the same time as we yell 'Baby Jordan' at the top of our lungs. Everybody got it?" All the little heads nodded with enthusiasm. "Okay, now let's practice a few times..."

After I was pretty sure we would let our balloons go in unison, we walked out from under the canopy and into the mid-afternoon sun. The sky felt brilliant above us and we hip-hip-hurrayed together with gusto. When we finally belted out, "Baby Jordan!" we let the baby-blue balloons go and watched them rise. Holly's youngest child, Robbie, refused to part with his treasure and I thought, *That's just the way it should be. If Jordan were Robbie's age and with us now, he wouldn't want to part with his balloon either.*

I took a picture of the balloons as they floated away in a group, but I must have been distracted because I missed the next thing. I learned later that a red-tailed hawk blessed the balloon ceremony with his presence. He swooped down, seemingly from nowhere, and began soaring with the balloons.

When the balloons were out of sight, I realized I hadn't planned for what came next. How would we get the casket from the wicker table to the grave and how would we help Lynn, who still needed to stroke the soft gingham, to be ready to part with it? I hadn't thought of a ceremony to facilitate this part. At other funerals in our family, the casket already had been suspended over the grave. I was pondering my dilemma when Lynn's mother asked to speak with me privately. Her voice uncertain, she said, "I don't know about this, but Lynn wants to see the baby again. What do you think?"

This surprised me, both because I hadn't expected to open the casket again and because I knew Lisa was pushing her own limits to even bring it up. Once again, I was struck by her mother-love for Lynn. Her actions continued to back up her words that she wanted only what her daughter needed. "I don't know either," I said, "but I'm real familiar with that little body. I'll open up the casket and see what I think."

I lifted the small coffin from the table and carried it to a folding chair away from the crowd. Sending up a prayer for help, I opened the lid partway. Jordan's face was harder to look at than it had been before, but nothing else seemed to have changed. I pulled his blue beanie over his face and then arranged the items stored in the casket to form a tableau near the casket. It was the same one I had created the night before. When I finished, I nodded to Lisa for her to escort Lynn and George over.

I understood now why I hadn't sealed the casket the night before, even though a tube of glue was provided by the manufacturer. The viewing had been arranged quietly for George and Lynn, but a few others gathered. Among them were the two who most needed to be there, Justice and Donna. I watched both their faces as they studied the quiet little figure in the blue-and-white box. Donna stood by it for a long time. Then I knew that for them, too, our baby Jordan had become real.

We took more pictures and when it seemed right, I put the tableau items back in the coffin and closed the lid. Now it truly was for the last time. After that, I went to the worker who was waiting in the background and told him it was time to remove the boards covering the grave. We spoke Spanish and I said our family would stay to watch them fill in the grave. It was a Latin custom so no further explanation was needed. He called a helper to the site and they began pulling the boards off the opening. It had been dug twelve feet deep so that it could accommodate, in time, my mother's body as well. A long ladder leading down to the bottom already was in place.

Even with its protective white shell, the casket was handled easily by one person. George and Kenny carried it between them, however, as if it were filled with gold. They latched it into its cover and drawing on their shared military training, hoisted the white box as if to mount it on their shoulders. Then they walked it with great dignity to the deep opening beneath the tree. There a worker took it from them and passed it down to another standing halfway down the ladder. The second worker carried the small casket to the bottom and rested it on the floor of the grave. Then I passed out flowers, wanting to make sure everyone had a white carnation to toss into the grave.

As Justice lofted his flower onto Jordan's coffin, I saw his eyes begin to sparkle with new understanding. The workers had gone for an earth-moving tractor, but there was a shovel stuck in the mound of dirt beside the hole. I remembered how we had taken turns shoveling dirt onto a casket in Honduras and called Justice to me. I could tell by the light in eyes that this was work he needed to do and he attacked it with enthusiasm. One by one, other family members came to take turns as the workers purposefully delayed their arrival. Some of us clearly needed to do this work more than others. Elizabeth's youngest son practically vaulted over the grave to get to the dirt pile.

Something wonder-filled seemed to be creating itself right before my eyes. When the earth mover arrived and took over the task of filling the grave, I trained my camera on Justice. It was clear the earth-moving machine confirmed for Justice a deep sense that this work was important. He danced a little jig matched by the sparkle and intensity in his eyes. Later an earth-packing machine took over to tamp down the loose dirt with solid, manly motions that shook our feet. I thought Justice would levitate with delight if physics allowed it. And I knew that if Jordan had lived and could be the same age as Justice, the two of them would be dancing on the lawn together right now.

Justice's wonder at filling the hole and covering his little brother's dead body with dirt seemed a classic example of the sanity in the old rituals, ones our society is losing. There is a child inside most of us that needs to fill holes and cover bodies. And there is a grown-up in many of us that needs ceremonies to show us how to sit with our grief and wait for it become part of our joy.

When the earth-tamping machine was finished, we loosened flowers from their arrangements, covered the grave with them, and took group pictures by it. Then we circled the grave, held hands and said the Lord's Prayer. After that, we split up between people who needed to go home and those who could join our family at the restaurant.

Wayne, Kenny and I waited until everyone was gone, then checked to make sure nothing was left out of order. After that, Kenny asked to be left alone. He took a folding chair and sat beside Jordan's grave, looking out toward where the red-tailed hawk lived. As I left the cemetery, I took another photograph to treasure. This time it was framed from a distance. It was my last nugget of inspiration for the day. I went to Olive Garden, allowed myself to be seated with everyone else, and fell face-first into my empty plate. Wayne took me out to Elizabeth's van and I heard him laughing softly as I passed out.

Chapter 16

❀ ❀ ❀

My three siblings came home with us after the dinner at Olive Garden. I was too tired to do more than bask in their light, but it felt luxurious having them all together under my roof. I put them all to bed in my living room where they had a sibling sleepover that night.

The children in my birth family were divided between the ones who sat around and the ones who ran around. The three older ones cogitated while the three younger ones got busy. When I awoke on Friday morning, I went to sit on the wraparound couch in our living room where my sisters had been sleeping. Helen was reading a book and Elizabeth was getting ready to pounce. Helen looked at Elizabeth and me and said, "I've just been having 147 deep thoughts before breakfast."

Elizabeth said, "Well, that's nice because I've been having about minus two!"

I laughed at them both and wondered how I possibly could love them more. Will was in the cocoon of bedding he had made for himself, still wedged between a table and a wall. As I looked at him, I thought of how he had joined his sisters the day before. I had teased him before the service about how he never sang with us. Then as we were singing "Kingdom Citizen," I heard his male voice in the background. The gesture felt very tender to me.

The next day, George, Lynn and the two kids came to stay with us for a week before returning home. Wayne and I were delighted to move out of our bedroom suite and allow them to use it. We weren't wealthy, but we felt rich at having something so nice and necessary to offer them. We put up a mattress in Wayne's office and felt like teenagers again sleeping on the floor.

I cared for George and Lynn as best I could throughout the following week. I knew enough about the statistics of infant death to know their marriage might be in for rocky times. I wanted to help them understand if I could that men and women tend to grieve differently. Particularly in a marriage, the man may tend his grief by giving his family the gift of his physical strength, getting back to work and trying to move things "back to normal." The woman may tend her grief by giving her family the gift of her emotional strength, drawing her family inward and knowing things never will be "normal" again in the same way as before. Both approaches are needed and both are worthy of respect. I was concerned that George wouldn't take enough time for his grief or give Lynn enough time for hers. I also was aware that Lynn could do the opposite.

I felt glad then when Lynn came to me one evening and asked to talk. I was not feeling well and so I was resting on Donna's canopied bed in her darkened room. Lynn came to sit on the floor beside me, later moving to lie down across the foot of the bed. "You know that conversation you would like to have with God?" she asked. "Well, I'd like to have it too."

I knew she was talking about the conversation in which nothing the One could say about why Jordan died would be good enough for me. "Yes," I said, and then just listened. When she stopped talking and waited for me to respond, I suddenly knew the answer. "I think if the One could be here in human form talking with us right now," I told her, "there wouldn't be any talking. There would be only weeping. I think Jordan's death makes the One just as sad as it makes us. I think everything is every bit as grief-stricken as we are. It's hard to understand this about the One because we tend to think only of words like *all-powerful, all-knowing* and *all-present.* But this is the essence of faith. It's living with the mystery and paradox of the deep things. It's about trusting the One that knew beforehand Jordan would not live out his years on this earth and yet still weeps over the fact that this is true."

Lynn and I talked for two hours. We talked mostly about what it felt like inside her to have her pregnancy terminated in such a violent manner. We talked about how no one, not even George, could enter fully into her grief because no one except her had really known Jordan. We talked about how her body did not know Jordan was missing and still tried to produce milk for him. We talked about how, baby in her arms or not, her body still would be post-partum. We talked about how hard it would be to meet people who had known she was pregnant and now asked about the baby. We talked about how Jordan never could be replaced and yet she still felt the need to hold an infant in her arms.

We talked about how hard it would be to encounter babies and women with babies for a long time to come. We talked about people who would prefer to be told she had only two children, who thought the best way to deal with Jordan's death was to pretend he didn't exist. We talked about the mystery of Jordan's death and how she would never know what had caused it and always would wonder if she had done something wrong. We talked about Jordan, what he would have been like, and how much we would miss him. "Sometime, maybe a year from now," I said, "you might want to talk about Jordan and think nobody remembers. Well, you can pick up the phone and call me because that little boy never will be far from his Nana's thoughts."

Lynn still was lying across the bottom of the bed as the conversation was winding down. She propped her head up on a hand ringed with double ID bracelets from the hospital and said, "I'm not the same person I used to be. I'm changed."

I said, "Yes. You are."

The next morning George and I went to the duck pond and had the same talk, although a different version of it.

As we watched children feeding the ducks, we asked the questions he needed to ask and said the things he needed to hear. When we were through, I felt safer for him. "My marriage will survive," he said, "because I'm a man who knows how to listen and I know how to change when I need to. I won't let my family suffer just because I'm too stubborn to work on myself."

I thought this was a good beginning and a good place for him to be. I knew that if he could allow broken spaces in his life, Spirit would come to him and fill them. I knew this was the way of the Spirit in the hard things. And I knew that this was Jordan's Road.

Jordan's Road is not the Jordan River. There is a difference. The former is a path leading from your past into your future, even though it winds and rarely proceeds in a straight line. The latter is a cataclysmic event, something that stands apart and does not lose its impact for the rest of your life. Because the Road winds around in turns and even circles, there will be more than one experience of crossing the River in your life. But each crossing leaves its own particular mark and after it has branded you, you never again are the same. Every crossing is a hard thing that changes you and if you allow it, frees you in some unalterable way. In the biblical account of the Exodus, the Jordan River was the dividing mark between the old place, the land of slavery, and the new place, the land of freedom.

In talking so much about the River, we sometimes forget there is a Jordan's Road. Or perhaps we do not even know. Jordan's Road is the path that prepares us for the River and then leads surely beyond its banks after the crossing. In life, this road leads to the death of our old selves so that new Life may be raised within us. All of us travel Jordan's Road, but few of us realize this. And so we do not know we are being prepared by the lessons of the Road to make each crossing of the River a joy-filled rather than a despair-saturated experience.

Instead, the River overwhelms us with its size when we reach it. And when we enter it, we struggle so hard against it that we cannot swim. We flounder and thrash about with such fury it's a wonder we manage to survive. We do not know how to breathe as we attempt to cross the River. We do not know how to float in the Presence that led us to the crossing. And so we are belched by the River out onto its banks and marooned there until we catch our breath. Sometimes we are so damaged by the crossing that we remain too long by the River in the hot sun and begin to rot.

The One is good, however, and Jordan's Road is not confined to the rigid timeline of our time-locked world. The things of Spirit operate in the realm of Spirit and tangible signs of Spirit's work are shrouded with mystery. They are not meant to be unraveled in a scientific sense. They are meant to be lived. At some point, our damaged and rotting selves move on. The call of the Presence is too great for us to remain forever by the River. And so we begin again the process of our own daily dying, reassured by the Presence of what our spirits know even as our bodies die. This is the way of Eternal Life.

It was common in Old Testament times to leave a pile of stones along the way to tell passers-by that, at a certain location along the road, the One had penetrated time and space and intervened in the affairs of humans. These piles of stone were telling stones. The stories in this book are some of my own telling stones. They tell portions of my journey down the Road and some of my crossings through the River. As I write these words and leave this particular collection of telling stones, it is important for me to know that I am moving away now from the banks of the River. I have been through the River many times and each crossing has changed my life, but I cannot continue from slavery to freedom if I stay where I land after a crossing. The freedom of any place along the Road becomes slavery if I remain too long.

I have been following the Presence since the beginning of my journey and I must follow it still. It is the Presence I seek, not the Road itself, and so I cannot remain on any portion of the Road longer than to erect a pile of stones and leave them as telling stones, as witnesses to those who, following the Presence, also pass by. This Presence sustains me along Jordan's Road from the beginning of my life here on earth to its conclusion, but it is not a stationary presence. The Presence moves, and I must follow with increasingly purposeful steps as I proceed steadily down the Road. Even now when I look back on a book titled after the most intense swim across the River of my life, I marvel at how much I have learned since making this specific pile of telling stones. But the Road is not the River. The Road began before the River was in sight and it continues now on into the horizon. When it will meet the River again I cannot know, and the end of it is never in sight.

This is a great mystery because the end of this Road, as of everything created, is the Presence from which I came, to which I will return, and in which I now travel. I am not in control of Jordan's Road and I do not know the ending or even the beginning. Because of this crucial fact, I cannot trust the Road itself. I must look only to the Presence that draws me and gives me courage to continue down a difficult road. This Road is the most painful one imaginable because it is all about my own death, about dying to those things I hold so closely, about saying yes to the Presence that I may live only in awareness of the One. This miraculous exchange of grace occurs again and again as I travel Jordan's Road, cross Jordan's River, and learn the way of Spirit in the hard things. And it is in this exchange that I find a most elusive truth. In the giving of my will to be taught by the lessons of the Road, I discover what I have always needed and yet has escaped my grasp. I give up control of my life and I am given, in return, my true self.

The End